JUMP

"This is a story of heartbreak but also of courage and hope. Diana's life has been so incredible in the way she has come from the confines of a religious philosophy so strict that her pastor actually successfully discouraged her from going to college, to an openness and awakening that is a beautiful thing to behold. Her heartbreak cracked her wide open, and rather than reverting into resentment and bitterness, she moved past all that into courage and hope and connection. I am honored to have been a part of her transformation."

—**Debra Stangl**
Founder, Sedona Soul Adventures

"A transparent, honest, authentic, and deeply emotional quest for truth…I know Diana well and over our 27-year relationship, have heard at least the headlines of this story, if not many of the details, and yet I am captivated and drawn in by her writing. I am deeply moved by the depth of her relationship with Spirit, the strength and joy she found in prayer, the intense ache and pain, and soaring heights of love and joy felt in her heart. I have been profoundly enriched through this beautiful labor of love… an exquisite gift to the world that has inspired renewed energy, desire, and zeal to find MY truth and authentic self."

—**Deby Beaty**
Certified Accunect Practitioner, LMT,
Reiki Practitioner

"*Jump Without Fear* invites us to look deeply and honestly at who we are and what we create with our actions in the world. In times like these of ever-increasing divisiveness, dehumanization of others, and disconnection from the natural world we must investigate our beliefs and assumptions. Yet many lack the moral grit and ethical guts to look at themselves. Diana shares her journey of introspection and self-expression with devotion, grace, and humility. She rediscovers the everlasting truth that every human has the ability to connect directly to the Divine to understand truth by its resonance and to be loved."

—**Christina Lee Pratt**
Teacher, Author, Healer,
and Founder of Last Mask Center

JUMP

A Memoir of Love,

WITHOUT

Loss, and Liberation

FEAR

Diana Brown Schmidt

Copyright © 2022 by Diana Brown Schmidt
Independently published

All rights reserved. No part of this publication may be reproduced, stored in a retrieval system, or transmitted in any form or by any means, electronic, mechanical, photocopying, recording, or otherwise, without the prior written permission of the copyright holder, except brief quotations used in a review.

Edited by Lorraine Anderson
Cover and Interior design by KUHN Design Group
Cover art by Wendybyrd Smith

ISBN 979-8-44395-141-6

*I dedicate this book to the eternal, infinite, creative Spirit
that never fails, never ends, and loves us all.*

*"It is so important not to keep what you know and who you are just a
tidy little secret between you and yourself, hunching over it protectively
as if it were the most tremulous candle flame always in danger of being
blown out, but instead to let it fan out into the world and into the lives
of others who, just maybe, could use the illumination themselves."*

GREGG LEVOY, *Vital Signs*

Contents

Introduction: A Surprising Awakening 9

MY SPIRITUAL ROOTS

1. Into the Fear Corral 17
2. Lessons in Trust 29
3. Healing Miracles 41

MY TREASURY OF LOVE

4. Desires of the Heart 57
5. Dark Night of the Soul 69
6. Words from a Prophet 81
7. Shaken to the Core 95
8. Ready to Love Again 107
9. Newlywed to Newly Widowed 121

SEDONA SOUL ADVENTURE

10. Breaking a Pattern 137
11. Paradigm Shift 151
12. Breathwork and Journey 163
13. Return to Joy 175

BACK HOME

14. Flowing with the Energies 191
15. In Search of Truth 209

Epilogue: All One in Love 225

Acknowledgments 229
References and Recommended Reading 231
Diana's Videos 235
About the Author 237

INTRODUCTION

A Surprising Awakening

This book is not the one I set out to write.

I intended to focus on my experience that Spirit is real and to give examples of the help that has arrived when I have prayed for it. I place a high value on peace making and did not want to offend anyone in my former church community. But then in browsing a bookstore one day I found myself drawn to the memoirs of people who were labeled heretics by religions they had left behind. It was like a light switch going on. I realized that I feared being authentic because I didn't want to face the repercussions. I understood that I was just continuing in a habit that had been well honed by my five decades as an evangelical Christian—my habit of being afraid to declare my own truth.

I understood that in writing my book I had been trying to skip over how stunned and horrified I had felt when I realized for the first time that some of the beliefs I had built my life on were no more than the opinions of others, and when I realized that these opinions had limited my growth and kept me from resolution of painful losses in my life. And I understood that I could not do that anymore.

At one time, I would not even read other sources that did not fit into my religious beliefs. I am acquainted with translations of scripture that are used to encourage shutting one's mind to every voice in the universe except those that conform to specific doctrinal beliefs. But I now know that you don't have to close your mind and put on blinders to protect yourself from error. That kind of thinking is based in fear.

Those who knew the old Diana might be shocked to read this book. Once, I was considered a leader in my church and admired for my faith and strength. I lifted others. Now, I can no longer be what I was then. Pushed by pain and pulled by curiosity, I have experienced a surprising awakening. This book is the story of that awakening.

FLOWING WITH THE CHANGES

Life has a way of interrupting our well-planned course. We have all heard stories of how life tragically interrupted someone's plans. We feel the pain of the professional dancer who was injured and will never be able to dance again. Our hearts go out to the surgeon who went blind. Life-altering experiences require us to make decisions and flow with the changes.

I responded to a life-altering experience by jumping from the familiar into the unfamiliar, by jumping out of my religious box searching for answers. I had not found the answers by continually repeating what was familiar to me. It seemed logical to me that I needed to look for answers in places I had never ventured to go. I was curious about what others had found that could be beneficial. What I discovered shook my religious foundations. I thought my foundations were firm, immovable. I knew what I believed and I trusted those beliefs and honored them with my lifestyle and my heart.

The unraveling and restitching of my belief system was an up-and-down yet ultimately enriching journey. The ups brought so much relief, joy, freedom, and expansion into my life that it was impossible for me to return to where I had started from. My relationship with Spirit grew even stronger as a result.

July of 2017 is when I came to a fork in the road. I was sixty-seven years old. It had been four months since my second husband, Mark, died suddenly. I was struggling with the abrupt transition from newlywed to widow in one short year. Grief, confusion, anger, and fear—emotions I didn't want to have—kept surfacing again and again. All the unresolved grief of my father's suicide, my loss of a foster child, and my first husband's sudden death had come back with a vengeance. It was much more than I could handle gracefully, and I was overwhelmed. I would weep with the pain of a broken and hurting heart. Under it all, I felt huge anxiety shaking my foundations. And adding to my fear was a fear produced by religious teachings.

I thought about the pain Jesus had suffered. He had lived a selfless life of service and good works. He did what was best for all, and he made it clear that God loved everyone. His life was inspiring; I admired Jesus and had often told God I wanted to serve others in any way I could. Despite his exemplary life, Jesus experienced horrific pain. Even when he knew that he was going to be crucified, he prayed a selfless prayer. He said, "Not my will but thine be done." I realized how weak I felt because of my losses. My courage to be as selfless as he was, paled in the face of fear.

I had reached my limit of submission. Out of fear that more pain might come my way, I made my request: "God, I know I said I would do anything for you. I take it back; I realize that I don't have that kind of strength. I am afraid. Please, no more, no more!"

I was angry—angry that I was ill-equipped and my beliefs were not adequate. The bulk of my life, I had relied on a belief system that had failed me in my darkest hours. Religious doctrines had convinced me that a good attitude toward all events was the right way to respond. I raised my head to address the invisible witnesses in the spirit realm and said, "I know I am failing this course, but I can't help it. I am so angry, so disappointed, and I don't know how to change that."

I began to fill the void in my life by reading books from Mark's library, encountering a vast amount of information that was new to me. Mark's books were not Bible-based; they fit into the metaphysical category. I read about labyrinths, meditation, shamans, reincarnation, life after death, and spiritual encounters that others had had with the universe. My understanding and worldview began to expand. I wanted to find the bliss and peace other people had found through meditation and journeys within themselves.

Journeying into higher consciousness and self-realization was a new concept to me. Paramahansa Yogananda's writings opened my awareness; his beliefs, experiences, and conclusions were remarkably similar to things Jesus had said. He and Jesus both taught that the door to the spirit realm is within us. The doctrines of an angry God, punishment, and hell were conspicuously absent from Yogananda's autobiography. He wrote, "The teachings of Jesus have been grossly misunderstood."

The writings gave me hope that there were people who could help me deal with grief and loss. The teachings that had formed me during my fifty years in the church had not been able to fill this void in my soul. I began to believe that I needed to step outside the religious corral where I had confined myself. Jesus said there is a kingdom within, and I went seeking that kingdom of peace. I thought, Surely God has made a way to fill the emptiness and brokenness within my soul. I want to find it.

And find it I did.

※

LIFE BROUGHT NEW PERSPECTIVES

I'm well aware of how others in my former congregation might see me now. They might pity me for being led astray, feel horrified that I would dare to suggest that the Bible is not the infallible word of God, or point to my second marriage as the beginning of my fall from the truth. The whole concept that an individual can be led by Spirit outside of the Christian church is a blaring fallacy to those within the walls.

I know of pastors who failed because they tried to follow the template of the church structure, which requires charisma to draw a crowd and the ability to raise funds to survive. These men could probably have flourished had they gone solo, led by Spirit. I know of people who served faithfully in the church but found that it was not and could not be enough to meet them in their hour of need. These people, like me, would be better off being guided by that which is perfect, the Spirit within, rather than by humans in a religious structure who are not perfect.

I respect the sincerity and devotion of those I knew in the church. I also know of some of the wounds they have suffered by trying to find their place in the church. I know of the casualties inflicted by fear-based dogma within my religious community. My heart longs to help those injured by such dogma to find freedom if they desire it.

That is why I'm telling my story. I want to share a perspective that was key to setting me free from grief. The fear-based dogma fell because it *felt good* to topple it; it brought relief. Replacing the heaven-hell story with the theory of reincarnation, a theory that was completely left out of my theological palette, is what gave me peace. Those who believe that if it is not in the Bible it has no merit cannot accept this, but it is my truth.

RESPECT AND HONOR

Throughout my life, I have had beautiful experiences with the powerful energy that is our universe. My interactions with Spirit have developed a strong faith in and love relationship with this all-encompassing power. I have kept a daily journal of those delightful guiding interactions for nearly forty years. Sometimes, it is a loving inner voice that whispers to me. The inner voice always speaks the perfect words of wisdom, comfort, and guidance that I need. At other times a vision appears on the blank screen of my mind, communicating in ways words cannot. Many times I have prayed and followed the wisdom downloaded to my mind and heart. As my life has moved forward, I have seen that the guidance from Spirit is always reliable and for my highest good.

When I was considering how to refer in this book to that which is infinite and unseen, I realized that it is essentially unnameable even though it has been referred to by many names. My earliest teachers called it God or Father God. Later, in the churches, I developed a relationship with Jesus and the

Holy Spirit. The Great Mystery is what Native Americans call it. Others have called it the Light, All That Is, Spirit, Source, the Universe, and the Divine.

When someone selects a name for it, that name becomes sacred to them. The name is a bonding point for the seeker. It is a way to address Spirit when speaking. I respect and honor any and all names people have chosen to call it, with the understanding that we are all referring to the same underlying reality. Deepak Chopra wrote, "Humans have a direct connection to a higher power, higher intelligence if they only turn to it. Spirit is just another name for pure infinite, eternal consciousness, but names don't matter. The support of spirit is real, you can test it for yourself."

Over the years, I have tested the source of my inner guidance many times. I have experienced many things that have illuminated my understanding, blessed my life, and showed me that the support of Spirit is real. In writing this book, I have decided to jump without fear again and share my story for the benefit of those who might find my experiences helpful. I desire to contribute to the energy of love and unity in our world. I desire to cut the cords of fear that suppress joy, growth, and discovery. I desire to honor the Source that guides all of us.

May you find the courage you need to follow your own authentic path. May our love and unity cause all the walls of fear to fall. We can co-create a wonderful world together. If every person lived without fear and became filled with the light of joy, peace, love, and harmony, our world would thrive. May my story be one strand of light toward that end.

My Spiritual Roots

1

Into the Fear Corral

When I was fourteen, a freshman in high school, I looked out my bedroom window into the night sky. The air was crisp and clear; the constellation Orion was in full view, surrounded by many twinkling stars. As I gazed at the scene, I imagined the enormity of the universe and wondered if God saw me. In comparison to that enormous vastness that had no limit, I felt so small and unseen. I imagined that I must be like the tiny round head on a sewing pin compared to the universe.

My perception of God at that time was that he was very busy and very far away. I had pieced together the fragments of information I had heard about God. People spoke as though God were male, similar in bodily form to us, but perfect, all-powerful, omniscient, omnipresent, and no doubt, enormous. This unseen Spirit was "up there," and we were "down here." I thought people met him when they died. I had heard people say if you were good, you went to heaven, and if you were not good, you went to hell, and it was God who had the final say on where you went. It seemed clear to me that God was critical and punished error.

There was a deep need within me for a close friend and wise counselor I could trust who would help me navigate life with wisdom. I longed for someone who understood me, who could read my thoughts, even when I had no words to express myself. I looked into the sky and released my first prayer of the heart. I imagined my words traveling upward to a place worthy of a king. I wondered if God would hear me. "God, I know you understand that I want to do the right things. I know you can see my heart. Please help me."

THE LOVE CIRCLE

I was the only girl in a family of five children. I often watched my parents hugging and kissing each other. I remember my father's eyes when he looked at my mother, and how she greeted him when he came home from work. It was evident they loved each other. I knew they loved us kids, but they did not hug and kiss us. There were no intimate one-on-one talks. I was aware of my inner sadness but did not understand why I felt that way. Hugs and long conversations with someone who made me feel understood, loved, heard, and valued would have helped me, but that insight came later; during childhood, I just knew an emptiness was there inside me.

I never developed a close bond with anyone during my growing-up years. Although I had what most would consider an idyllic childhood—with acres of nature to play in, a stable home life, extended family support, neighbors and pets, summers of camping—I had a feeling of being on the outside, a feeling I described to myself as being outside the love circle. Somehow, my mother had concluded that I did not want her to cuddle and hold me when I was a little child. My father was a quiet, good man who rarely communicated. I do not fault either of my parents for failing to meet my needs for physical affection and heart-to-heart talks; like all parents, they did the best they knew how. They were parenting in the same style their parents had used: patriarchal rule with discipline or punishment as a remedy.

My parents had not received what they needed as children, and without a handbook explaining a better way to parent children, they mimicked their childhood training as faithfully and lovingly as they knew how. They expressed their love for us by modeling integrity, sacrifice, and hard work. They often denied themselves to provide for us children. They demonstrated a strong work ethic, honesty, and loyalty to a spouse. We learned to respect elders, obey the rules, and say memorized prayers at dinner and bedtime. I learned to work, do what was right, and obey authority.

My two smiley-faced uncles lifted the boredom of family reunions for me; they were friendly to us children and understood our shyness. They would stride over with happy grins on their faces and hug a child who was standing on the sidelines. I was so grateful for their hugs. One summer, I was a guest at a cousin's house for a few days. My uncle was generous with hugs, conversation, and big smiles, and I felt happy and welcome while at their home. When they drove me back home to my parents, I was surprised that I felt sadness as I waved and watched their car drive away. I did not understand why my heart sank; I'm home, I thought to myself, so why do I feel sad?

I tried to be perfect but was not. I was very gullible and naive and made mistakes. I learned that making mistakes would subject me to scolding or punishment. I felt deep pain when criticized for my failings; it seemed unfair to me. My logic was this: if I had known in advance that my choice would lead me toward error and failure, I would not have taken the wrong route. I reasoned that I would have made better choices if my parents had given me better instructions. If they had talked to me and explained things, I would have been wiser. I felt the lack of parental intimacy and understanding.

Emotionally, I felt myself being excluded farther and farther outside the love circle—the bond I saw between my parents. I wanted someone to look at me the way my father looked into the eyes of my mother. I wanted guidance to help me navigate life. I wanted a friend I could trust, one I could confide in, one who would understand even when I messed up and would know that my original intent was to do the right thing.

By age fourteen, life had conditioned me to believe that marriage was the ultimate prize, the optimum relationship where people felt loved and special. I concluded that I needed to be perfect or people would be disappointed or angry with me, that breaking rules and making mistakes would bring criticism and punishment. I believed that people could not understand my heart, so it was better to keep my own counsel and not confide in or depend on others. I believed that only God understood my confusion and my desire to do right.

I decided that I was willing to earn my way into the love circle, and I thought perfection, obedience, integrity, and wisdom were the entry keys.

※

INTRODUCTION TO RELIGION

When I was a junior in high school, I remember making a comment that revealed my concept of God being "up there." After class, a student who had heard my statement approached me and invited me to come to his church. He indicated that if I did, it would change my understanding of God.

Two of my girlfriends and I went together to visit his church. The Gospel of Christ Tabernacle was a little church set out in the countryside. From the very beginning, it was evident to me that this church was different from any others I had attended. The music was uplifting, and the people sang with conviction, joy, and enthusiasm. The songs spoke of a relationship with Jesus and God. My parents had taken me and my siblings to a Presbyterian Sunday school during the summer months, and it was nothing like this church.

The pastor asked the congregation if anyone had a testimony they wanted to share. Having a "testimony" was a new concept to me. One after another, people stood up in their pews and shared how God had answered their prayers. They said he had met their needs, healed their sicknesses. I could tell these people had a relationship with him; he was not "up there" but "down here" and very much in their lives. It was the first time in my life that the name *Jesus* connected to my awareness. It was there that I heard his name and realized people could know him. They talked about "being saved." I heard them pray in unrecognizable languages, something they called "speaking in tongues." I was in a whole new world with a different kind of people.

After the service there was an altar call, and I timidly approached the pastor and asked, "How do you get saved?" Dressed immaculately in a buttoned-up vest, bright-colored shirt, and tie, he had wavy, stark white hair and a powerful voice. It was evident that he enjoyed being the center of attention and the authority. He handed me a book titled *So Great Salvation* and said it would help me and answer my questions.

Hooked and hungry for more, I wanted what these people had. I wanted a friend who understood me, who could advise me. I wanted God, salvation, and Jesus. These people were interacting with God, and he was responding to them. The God of the sky had come down to earth where I could reach him. My girlfriends were not impressed by the church service and had no desire to continue attending. My response was entirely different. Something inside me wanted God, and it seemed these people had found the pathway to him.

At home, I gobbled up the information in the book the pastor gave me. I followed the instructions in the book, and in the privacy of my bedroom I began praying and asking God to save me. I was ignorant of the ways of Spirit. I did not know that as soon as I called, he would answer. I kept praying and asking and praying and begging for him to "save" me. I did not know what to expect. My life interactions had always been with human beings. I could not see God or hear him, so I did not know if he heard me. I knew nothing of the concept of faith.

I went to the youth meeting the following Saturday night. The pastor immediately saw the change in me and told me that I had gotten "saved." He told me that I had been "born again." That began my spiritual journey. It also began the pattern of getting all my understanding through a pastor of a church. I became dependent on the pastor to explain what was happening in my spiritual life.

The truth is that the years I depended on that pastor nearly destroyed me.

OBEYING AUTHORITY

I had no idea how to hear God for myself. The pastor identified himself as a prophet. He would pray in tongues, and a hush would fall over the congregation. Everyone would wait in anticipation. Then in a loud, powerful voice, he would speak the "interpretation" in English so we could understand the mysterious message. The pastor called this ability an anointing. He told stories of people who had received miraculous healings when he and others prayed. Often the interpreted messages scolded people. It seemed God was often angry, and it frightened me.

Bible verses reinforced the concept that laypeople needed teachers. The pastor preached that people ordained by God were to teach and lead laypeople. Those individuals who were called apostles, pastors, prophets, teachers, and evangelists had elevated status in the church. As I listened to the teachings and read the Bible, I tried to find my place. To my understanding there was a clear hierarchy, and I was on the bottom. The pastor taught that the Bible was the infallible word of God. Proof that we were not to question a pastor's authority was in this "infallible" word. He emphasized Psalm 105:15, "Touch not my anointed and do my prophets no harm."

I was very gullible and naive at the tender age of sixteen. I believed I was to obey authority. That meant obey the pastor, this prophet, who God had ordained to the ministry. I reasoned that if God chose him, it must be the right thing to do. More than anything else, I wanted God to love me. I wanted to do the right thing and to please him. I was back to my childhood need for love and my conditioning to obey authorities. Be perfect, be obedient, and you will be loved and not punished. Follow these teachings and you will not go to hell. Church doctrines created real fear in me. At the time, I thought I was respecting the highest authority.

I listened to everything the pastor taught and altered my life to fit my new understanding of God. My parents and classmates commented, "You are different; you have changed." An older teenage girl in the youth group I attended watched me bubbling over with enthusiasm for God. She spoke to me with evident disgust, "It will wear off." I immediately understood that hers had worn off, but I knew my own heart, and she was wrong. I said nothing in return, but I thought, even here in church, people criticize. I withdrew my trust in people once again. I decided, keep your own counsel, keep your joys to yourself. The practice of keeping my feelings a secret became a pattern, a pattern of self-protection. I was going deeper into being a people pleaser and losing touch with myself.

My thirst for God never ended; I loved him. I loved the sections in Psalms and Proverbs that taught wisdom. I loved the passages in the Bible that showed how loving God was. I did not understand the bloody sacrifices or the killing. The scriptures portraying God as angry, jealous, and vengeful baffled me. But I dismissed my concerns because, after all, God is perfect; what do I know.

The pastor taught me that I needed to give up my will to follow God's will, but I found this concept very difficult. How could I know what to do if I shut off my ideas, interests, and inner nudges? I struggled with my desires, thoughts, and intuition. At times I thought, this is crazy; it makes me feel brain dead. I tried to quiet myself so that I could hear what God wanted me to do, but it seemed so difficult. Heavy, oppressive emotion filled my heart as I struggled to block out my thoughts and will. I was killing my own inner guidance because I thought that was what I was supposed to do. A scripture in the Bible, 1 Corinthians 15:31, encourages people to die to themselves; it says to die daily. I was trying very hard, and at times it did feel like death.

※

Being hungry to learn about God, I went to the local library and asked the librarian for books about religion. I was naive and did not know there were many religions, and most were not in agreement with each other. I thought everyone who loved God would love each other. The librarian directed me to the religious books section. I selected a book about Edgar Cayce and read the book with amazement at his ability and method. I was so grateful that God had given him this unique ability to help others. People would come to him with illnesses, hoping that he would be able to prescribe a cure. Cayce would lie down, close his eyes, and go into a meditative state called a trance. While in a trance, he was able to diagnose illnesses. Through him came holistic formulas that helped people get well.

To my understanding, he had a special gift from God. Edgar Cayce accessed the spirit realm and received prescriptions that helped people. I shared what I had been reading with the church pastor. To my surprise, he informed me the church frowned on this method of healing people. I realized that the church did not accept supernatural events outside its doctrines. This logic seemed strange to me. Hundreds were healed by following the prescriptions they received from Edgar Cayce.

The pastor warned me to stick with the Bible and stay away from that type of book. He said healings that came through individuals, like Edgar Cayce, were white magic and designed to lead people astray. Even worse, deceiving demons might be behind the healings. Well, I did not want to get in trouble with God, so I quit reading books that were not Bible-based.

Bit by bit, I continued shutting down my intuition and deferring to the words of others. I erected a mental corral and told myself to stay inside this corral, stick with the Bible. The corral of fear and diminishing self-worth had a firm grip on me. I feared grieving God, feared being led astray, feared mistakes, feared breaking the rules, feared punishment, and feared trusting my intuition. Fear stacked upon more fear.

A year had passed since I asked Jesus into my life. It was my senior year of high school, and I planned to go to college and get a teaching degree. I wanted to become a physical education teacher. I had an ingrained aversion to office work; the last thing I ever wanted to do was to sit behind a desk all day. I was a country girl at heart; all of nature enthralled me. The smell of fir trees, dirt, and fresh air combined with the exhilaration of working under the warm sunshine was an elixir to me. My body liked to move; I was happiest on my feet, enjoying the feel of muscles gaining strength. That is why I wanted to teach physical education. I envisioned teaching track, softball, and other outdoor activities.

I attended a youth group at the pastor's home on Saturdays, and he heard about my plans to go to college. He told me to stay at the church and not go to college. He said the college would erode my faith, and I needed to become more grounded in the faith. I trusted him and did as he told me. In one short year, I had become thoroughly indoctrinated and devoted to Bible teachings and the church hierarchy. My brain and intuition were not allowed. I was dependent on church teachings and providential circumstances to navigate life.

My mother tried to persuade me to go to college as planned. The lack of bonding and parental counseling during my earlier years prevented me from trusting her judgment. The pastor had stepped into my life as God's authority. I thought I was following God by obeying the pastor. I did not know how to hear God's voice for myself, so I listened to the pastor rather than my parents. It pained me deeply knowing that not going to college hurt my parents, and I muffled the tears that often fell when I was alone in my bedroom.

I graduated from high school and found seasonal work with a family friend who owned a megafarm. My job was to oversee transitory workers in his berry fields. As workers arrived, I checked their Social Security cards to be sure their names were on the farm's legitimate workers list. I inspected berry rows to insure workers were picking them clean. As I weighed and stacked full berry crates on the cannery truck, I gained muscle. The daily sunshine gave me a glorious tan. I enjoyed every day in the fields and fresh air.

I purchased a car with my summer earnings. With no college training on my schedule, I started looking for work. The pastor told me that God opens and shuts doors. If God opened a door, I was to enter. It did not matter that the last place I wanted to be was working in an office and sitting at a desk. I took the first job I was offered, working in downtown Portland at Credit Bureau Metro. It was an office job, sitting behind a desk.

I found an apartment and began my solo journey. I left home quickly because I was grieving deeply and privately, knowing my decisions were hurting my parents and brothers. Every time I was with them, I would feel their distress. When I would visit them, tears would be streaming down my face as soon as I got back into my car to drive back to my apartment. I loved my family, but I did not know how I could please them and please God simultaneously. I did not even consider the reality that I was not pleased. Christians were supposed to suffer for their faith. I felt my only alternative was to follow what the pastor taught, which I equated with following God.

I rebuked myself for having any ideas about running my own life. Turmoil filled my heart as I used every bit of my willpower to obey the pastor's directives. When I heard the pastor teach that Christians should not fellowship with unbelievers, who were destined to go to hell, my emotional pain compounded. According to that teaching, all of my family were unbelievers because they had not followed the church's doctrines, which would make them "saved." I was sick at heart over this dilemma but hoped God would be merciful and save my family. I reasoned that if I were obedient and prayed for them, they would all get saved and not have to go to hell.

I was miserable, but I thought I was obeying God. I cried constantly. Ironically, my parents were the ones who had taught me to obey authority. I was in a situation where I had to choose who the highest authority was, God or my parents. God was the highest authority. I was bound to obedience and to the pastor I thought was God's prophet. Fear ruled my life.

✤

As I learned more of the religious rules, I diligently adjusted my life to conform. I am a scholastically inclined person and studied my Bible, believing it would guide me through life and every situation. One Bible verse made me think that all earthly honors were distasteful to God. Philippians 3:8 says, "I counted all but dung save for the knowledge of my Lord and Savior Jesus Christ."

I looked at all the awards and accolades I had earned during my high school years. My yearbook contained a photo of all the class officers; I was the class secretary. I had National Honor Society pins and a John Philip Sousa award for playing first chair coronet in the band for four years. I reasoned that if God considered honors as dung, I should not keep these reminders. I felt a little bit sick as I began throwing out all the things that had validated my life efforts. My belief that authorities and older people knew better than I had far-reaching effects.

Certainly, if God chose pastors to lead others, they must be people of integrity. Right? He knew best.

✤

I had no TV, no radio, and no trusted adults outside of the church. As year followed year, I focused on studying my Bible. The bulk of my religious guidance came from the charismatic pastor of the little country church. His fancy two-tone shoes would click, click, click as he strode up to the pulpit. He told stories of miracles and his encounter with an angel.

The supernatural was new to me. The pastor and his wife often lamented that today's churches lacked the miracles and power of God. Their longing for the miracles of yesterday caused me to conclude that today's churches were somehow failing. They told of their experiences during the 1949 revival in Portland, Oregon, led by healing evangelist William Booth-Clibborn. Miraculous healings occurred, and Booth-Clibborn's charismatic teaching held people spellbound. My pastor said he received his anointing at that time and was a key player during the revival.

Sermons and stories continually reinforced my fear. The pastor told a story about two young men who had mocked a minister of the gospel and blocked the tailpipe of his car by stuffing it with debris. After this disrespectful deed, the two young men left for a drive in their car. En route, they drove through a stop sign masked by overhanging branches. Another vehicle broadsided them, and they were both decapitated in the wreck. The story implied that God was judging the young men because they had "touched" his prophet. I was petrified.

The pastor read a story in 2 Kings 2:23. Young men were disrespecting the prophet Elisha, telling him to take off into the heavens in a chariot of fire like his predecessor Elijah had. They said, "Go up, you baldhead; go up, you baldhead." Then Elisha turned around, looked at them, and called down a curse on them in the name of the Lord. Suddenly two female bears came out of the woods and mauled forty-two of the young men.

These stories fanned my fear of God and prophets. I was only seventeen years old, and the bars of my fear corral grew stronger and taller. I was determined to be obedient and stay inside that corral. I was compliant to the rules, and yes, I was adhering to my understanding of "dying daily" as advised by scripture. I worked hard at conforming, relinquishing all my power, and ignoring my mind and heart. Conditioned from birth to obey authorities and please people, I stayed in the suffocating web of religion that had usurped control. I had lost my self-steering capacity and given up my desires. I was a puppet on a string.

Although I had no way of realizing it at the time, my conditioning and my trusting, naive beliefs were setting me up for years of emotional pain.

2

Lessons in Trust

My father worked at Reynolds Metals, an aluminum plant, and also farmed our twenty-acre homestead. He had planted a field of raspberries and was under contract to deliver his berries to the cannery. Another buyer tried to persuade my father to sell some of the berries to him. Dad refused the offer and told the buyer he was under contract. The hopeful buyer replied, "No one would know." My dad replied, "I would." He modeled integrity. I grew up thinking the majority of people were like my dad. I transferred the respect and trust I had for my dad to others. I expected others to do the right thing.

After I left home to work and live on my own, it did not take me long to realize I needed to reserve my trust for those who earned it. I was perplexed. How would I know in advance which people had pure, honest motives? One day I read this scripture: "Blessed are the pure in heart, for they shall see God." I latched onto that concept and decided, yes, that was what I needed. If a pure heart could see God, surely it could know who was to be trusted. I wanted a pure heart so people could not deceive me. I knelt down on my knees in my apartment and asked God to give me a pure heart. As I prayed, my heart felt like it was breaking. I cried many tears and repeated my request over and over.

After that night of asking and tears, something changed in me. I noticed I had a strong aversion to violence, especially in films where people hurt each other. I became aware that I could see the underlying motives in people. I could see the good in people even when they could not see it in themselves. I saw past their anger and into their pain and need for love. It was as though I saw what God saw in them, and I loved them as they were. When I later became a store manager responsible for hiring and training staff, my intuition enabled me to scan people accurately. I had an inner knowing which people would fit in with the rest of the employees. My team all worked in harmony with each other.

One day, a minister's wife approached me and told me about an unusual ability she had. She occasionally had spiritual sight and saw what others could not see. She told me a story to illustrate. A man was talking to her and trying to negotiate a deal. With her spiritual sight, she could see a black box on the man's forehead. It was a warning to her, and not long afterward, the deceit of the man became apparent. She then told me, "I have seen a white heart on your forehead."

My mind flashed back to the intense prayers when I asked God for a pure heart. My request for a pure heart had manifested in my life.

DYING DAILY

As I entered my early twenties, I watched other young women my age marry and have children. The pastor convinced me that I needed to refrain from dating, stay in the church, and learn more about God's ways. I followed the path of my conditioning and obeyed authority. Laypeople in the church were considered sheep. Pastors were the shepherds, and sheep were to follow the shepherd's guidance. My heart sank deeper into sadness as each year passed, and I waited for God to move me forward. I wanted out, but church doctrines and the minister's words had convinced me that what I was feeling was rebellion against God.

I worked hard at following the rules, ignoring my "rebellious" heart and trying to be submissive so I could discern what God required of me. I learned that tithing was an important discipline for anyone who was committed to serving God, so I gave 10 percent of my income to the church. As I look back at those days now, I see how manipulated I was. I supported the pastor and his wife financially while the pastor served himself and fed off my energy. He used his charisma and position to retain me under his control for his own purposes.

He had destroyed my plan to go to college. Instead, I had a job at Credit Bureau Metro, where every day was the same routine. We wore headsets and received calls fed to us by a switchboard. The calls were from clients who needed credit reports on people. On each call I parroted the words, "Credit Bureau Metro, operator 38, may I help you?" I would read the desired credit report to the client and then take another call. I never saw the customer; I was a voice speaking to another voice. I longed for physical activity, fresh air, nature, and interaction with others. I was doing what I had never wanted to do.

In the seventh year on that job, I became ill. The illness progressed until I was so weak that I could no longer work. Everything in my life was what I did not want. I felt trapped by religious rules and doctrines but feared breaking them. I grieved over the pain I had brought to my family. I had no one to confide in and did not know what to do. I was under the control of a pastor that I thought God had put in charge. I felt God did not value me very much, and I must have done something very wrong.

I went to doctor after doctor seeking help. Most of them told me my illness was all in my head. I grew thinner and thinner; my weight dropped to ninety-eight pounds. The food I ate went through my body rapidly and provided little nourishment.

Being unable to work, I applied for welfare, and through welfare medical assistance I was able to see a specialist. On the day of my physical exam, I drank the barium shake they gave me and lay on an X-ray table in a hospital gown. The doctor stood beside me and guided my breathing so the X-rays would not be blurred. I was sure he had repeated those instructions hundreds of times. He spoke in a slow rhythm, "Don't breathe or move, don't breathe or move, don't breathe or move." I lay quietly on the table and waited while he looked at my X-rays.

"This is not normal," he said in a low murmur.

I glanced over at the white surface of the box displaying my X-rays. I wondered what his trained eye was seeing on those films. My mind shifted into action as I got up from the X-ray table and walked to the dressing room. Finally, something is evident, and I am going to get some answers. If I know what is making me sick, I can take appropriate action to get well.

Office staff led me down the hall and into a private room where the doctor sat behind his desk. His eyes met mine as I entered. I saw him studying my face and could feel an underlying tension. He indicated that I should sit in the stuffed chair facing his desk. His voice was low and solemn. "You have an incurable disease, known as Crohn's disease; it is a terminal illness. We can try medicines, but there is no guarantee that your body will respond to them. I can also recommend dietary guidelines for you to follow. We don't know any methods to stop the advancement of this disease. You should inform your family and make preparations to die."

I was twenty-seven years old. My body was weak, but my heart responded like a lion. I listened in silence and inwardly said, No! I am not going to die. For ten years, I had been trying to be obedient to teachings based on scripture. I had submitted myself, trying to "die daily" to my own will, desires, ambitions, goals, and dreams. Now, my body was dying.

I went to the pastor, and he prayed with me about my illness. He prayed in English, and then there was a shift to his spirit language. He prayed in tongues, a brief silence followed, and then he gave the "interpretation." The interpreted message was encouraging to me. This time there was no scolding, only comfort. I heard these words: *I am your physician. Wait upon me, and you will see my good hand.*

From that moment on, I *knew* I was not going to die.

JOURNEY TO HEALING

I received enough money through welfare to pay my rent and buy food. One thing I could still do was paint pictures. I had been painting and teaching myself how to use oil paints. I supplemented the welfare funds by selling my paintings. People liked my artwork and were grateful to purchase them at bargain prices.

I began the task of finding information about how to rebuild my health. I read self-help books that suggested methods for curing Crohn's disease. I went to an MD who had been raised and trained in the medical practices of India. His words encouraged me. He told me I could get well by following the protocol of cultivating a calm mind and eating whole foods. He said, "This illness is not incurable. Impaired digestion will improve if you eat one food at a time. Grate a carrot and eat it; when you get hungry again, steam a potato and eat it with a bit of butter. Focus on fruits and vegetables. If you eat bread, choose one that is a blend of grains, not whole wheat. Don't eat white flour or white sugar. Chew your food slowly." He gave me some homeopathic medicine in the form of tiny round pills.

I also went to a Western MD, who gave me drugs and dietary guidelines that included white sugar and low-fiber foods. These guidelines directly contradicted everything I was reading in the health books. I chose to follow the dietary guidelines from the Eastern MD. I cut out all sugar and processed foods and ate lots of vegetables. I took both the Western drugs and the Eastern homeopathic medicines.

It was 1977, and recognition of the mind-body connection was gaining ground, along with the health food movement. Reading and research opened my awareness to the link between my thoughts, emotions, and disease. For ten years, I had been unhappy and submissive to what I did not want. I did not need a therapist to tell me I needed to do things that would bring me joy. I worked on directing my thoughts and began happy heart and laughter therapy of my own making. I would go off by myself and skip and dance to make myself laugh.

Crohn's disease is challenging to turn around, and people have died trying. As I diligently followed my program to regain health, I gained strength and weight little by little. I had relapses but held on to the belief that I would get well. I focused on eating healthy food and thinking happy thoughts, one of which was that I was now free to find a job I enjoyed. From the day sickness had forced me to quit my job at the credit bureau, six months had passed.

Being on welfare had made it possible for me to get a medical diagnosis but also made me feel ashamed, and with my new knowledge about the mind-body connection, I knew those feelings were sabotaging my efforts to regain health. I believed that earning my way and getting off welfare would assist my recovery, so I planned to get a part-time job while I regained my strength.

I went to town and walked from store to store, filling out applications. The next day I got a call to come in for an interview. It was the store manager at Discount Fabrics (now JoAnn Fabrics). She was a Catholic woman who had twelve children of her own. I had noted on my application that I was not sure of my strength or endurance due to Crohn's disease. As she interviewed me, she shared that one of her daughters had the same illness. Her direct question revealed her firsthand knowledge of the challenge I was dealing with: "Do you think you can work?" Relieved that she understood my dilemma, I answered, "I don't know, but I have to try." She responded, "I will start you out on a very light schedule. Keep me informed how you are doing."

From the first day I started work, my body began healing. I loved working at the store; for me, it was like a playground. Every moment I was at work was a total joy. I was in a creative person's paradise, surrounded by beautiful fabric. I loved helping the customers find what they needed for their projects. This job was worlds away from the job I had left behind. I had spent seven years in a stuffy office building, sitting behind a desk. During that time, I had faced a computer and never saw the faces of the people I served. Even though my body and legs ached from standing on my feet for hours during my first week at the fabric store, I knew it would pass. Soon I was moving all day long, building muscle, and my mind and body loved every minute.

When the delivery truck arrived with new merchandise, it was like Christmas to me. The boxes came filled with crafts and exciting fabrics; my job was to help showcase the new items in the store. I marveled and felt so blessed to have a job that was like play to me. My heart was happy because I was interacting with people face to face. My body and soul started healing in leaps and bounds. I was where I belonged.

Within six months, I was promoted to store manager and began working full time. I continued climbing the ladder to regain my health. It took five years before tests showed there was no trace of Crohn's disease. Even today, many years later, I am free from this disease.

Later in life, I reflected on the events that had transitioned me from disease to health and from misery to joy. I remembered how my heart spoke loudly that office work was not what I wanted. I also remembered how the pastor had told me to walk through the doors that God opened. I chose to follow his words, and it was the wrong choice for me. I realized that I had been too compliant, submissive, and dependent on the opinions of others. My body did what it had to do to get me out of that job. It quit, collapsed, and forced me out. I am so grateful! I decided then that waiting until circumstances force you to action is lousy theology.

That brush with death helped me regain a small measure of my power. It helped me respect the language of my heart. It was an incremental step away from fear-based doctrines. I prayed with new understanding, "God, teach me to hear you so that my body doesn't have to go into death mode to get me to make changes in my life."

※

As my spiritual roots kept growing, some incidents gave me reasons to believe in angels. It has become my lifelong habit to thank them when their intervention seems apparent.

I was living in the city in an old building converted into separate apartments. It was the end of the workday, and I needed to cross a one-way street on my walk home to my apartment. I looked to my right, and no cars were coming, so I began walking across the street. Suddenly my body stopped moving forward. It was as though somebody flipped an OFF switch, and like a puppet on a string, my body became motionless. I had made no conscious effort to stop and had no physical sensation other than my body becoming immobile. At the exact moment I stopped, a car sped past me from the left, missing my body by a few inches. The young boys driving the car were going the wrong direction on a one-way street. Had I kept walking, their car would have hit me. Amazed and thankful, I credited the angels for intervening.

I have had many incidents in my life where I have exhausted myself trying to accomplish something. When I ask angels to help and the issue resolves, I say, "Thank you."

※

My battle with Crohn's disease had been at its peak in 1976 and 1977. In 1981, I was healthy and enjoying my job as a store manager. One day, I noticed that I could not hear well when I held the phone to my left ear. Incidents began to multiply, making it evident something was wrong with my hearing. A hearing test confirmed that I had a hearing loss in my left ear. My response was to spend hours in prayer asking for healing. I wondered if all the drugs I took during my episode with Crohn's disease had affected my hearing. As time went on, my right ear was also affected.

I periodically went for hearing tests and was alarmed to learn each time my hearing had grown worse. After another exam, the audiologist grew quiet and delayed his findings for a while. I recognized from his body language that he was hesitant to be the bearer of bad news. Finally he spoke. "You would be wise to learn sign language and prepare for employment that does not depend on your hearing. Your hearing is still deteriorating; you may go deaf." Fear moved in like a robber; I felt like someone had just amputated a part of my body. My hearing was my point of contact with the world. How could I survive without it? I could not imagine how terrible it would be to live in a world without sound.

An audiologist suggested hearing aids. I was stalling, hoping for a miracle of healing. I was only in my early thirties. I thought getting hearing aids was giving up on hoping for divine healing too soon. About that time, I was offered a promotion to district manager at JoAnn Fabrics. I was reluctant to give up my beloved job as the store manager and the family-like relationships I enjoyed with my employees. As I contemplated being a district manager, I faced reality; hearing loss impaired my ability to work in a retail environment.

District managers spoke with store managers in enclosed offices where the walls helped amplify the sound. I could hear reasonably well in those offices, so I accepted the promotion.

LOVE AND LOSS

Besides bringing the start of my hearing loss, 1981 held a shocking event that required me to face my greatest childhood fear, that I would lose the ones I loved the most. It also catapulted me back into touch with my family, from whom I had been estranged for years because of my pastor's influence.

My father was the youngest of six children. When he was six years old, his father died from complications of pneumonia. His mother never remarried, so my dad grew up without the role model of a father in the home. Dad served in the Navy and then met and married my mother. He was a good and faithful man, a hard worker, devoted to his wife and five children. Dad enjoyed farming his land, deer hunting, fishing, and camping. But sadly, during the many years that he worked for Reynolds Metals as a shop foreman with daily exposure to molten aluminum, he became ill due to exposure to the metal fumes.

The symptoms of his illness began manifesting about eleven years after I graduated from high school. His physical health and mental capacities began to decline. He had difficulty focusing and eventually had to quit his job. His mind troubled him, and he could not stop grinding his teeth at night. Doctors prescribed drugs that were supposed to help him but had a known side effect of causing people to be suicidal.

His symptoms grew worse, and his depression deepened. During this illness, he was in a mental ward for a short period to protect him from hurting himself. He had always been self-motivated and self-reliant, a provider, and he was deeply troubled at being unable to perform his household and provider duties. He was only fifty-nine years old and very ill. His entire life, he had found his value in sacrificing and providing for his family. He saw no value in himself when he could not work or provide for his family.

During the time of his illness, I was still managing the store at JoAnn Fabrics. One day while I was at work, I got a phone call from my brother. His voice was somber and direct, and his words seemed surreal: "Dad shot himself." There was a long silence between us as the shock of what he had just said penetrated my mind and heart. Hoping against hope, I asked quietly, "Is he gone?"

"Yes."

Horror and disbelief flooded me. There was no way I could continue working my shift. I told my assistant manager that she was in charge and headed out to my childhood home to see my mom. As I drove the car, I was screaming at the top of my lungs, "No, no, no!"

His death and the shocking way he left this earth marked me deeply. I experienced heavy grief. The heart pain was excruciating. I would see someone walking down the street who bore a resemblance to my dad, and all the emotions would flood to the surface. I did not know what to do with the feelings.

My father had become a Christian before he died and that was a comfort to me, but the years that my pastor's influence had kept us separated made me sad. At one time my pastor and my father had met, and my dad would not shake his hand. He said nothing, just turned and walked away. He thought it wrong that the pastor had separated his daughter from her family. As I was deep in mourning, the pastor implied to me that my father's death was God's judgment because he had disrespected a prophet (the pastor). This thought did nothing to console me but only reinforced my fear of God.

My father's death was the first profound, significant loss I had ever experienced in my life. As the years passed, the emotional pain would rise and fall at intervals. By the end of the fifth year it had lessened, but it never really left. It just simmered below the surface, masked by work and busyness.

※

INNER HEARING

As a district manager for JoAnn Fabrics, I traveled up and down the I-5 corridor daily. I had fourteen retail stores under my supervision, located throughout Oregon and Washington. My job was to visit each store twice a month.

While driving, I prayed; in the hotel rooms at night, I prayed. It was a season of intense prayer and many tears as I kept asking God to restore my hearing. I had seen miracles; I knew they happened.

Perusing a bookstore, I found a book titled *Hearing God* by Lory Basham Jones. From the moment I began reading it one night in my hotel room, it resonated with me. I had a deep hunger to experience what Lory had discovered. The book contained the day-by-day personal journal she had written during her prayer time. She would ask God a question and an inner voice would answer. Her journal contained the question she asked and the answer she received. She kept the journal for her benefit and had no intention of publishing it. But then her husband, actor Dean Jones, read her journal and found that the answers spoke to his heart also. Dean knew the journal could benefit others and encouraged Lory to publish it.

Dean was right; I was one of those who benefited from reading Lory's book. It became a life changer for me. The words God had given to Lory were also speaking to my life. Divine guidance and wisdom are always right on target. I started a journal, asking God my questions. It surprised me how well I could hear the answers. The best part was the *love* and kindness in the answers. The guidance was perfect, exactly what I needed each time. Like Lory's journal, the words from the inner voice met the needs of a human heart.

I was grateful that hearing loss had motivated me to spend so many hours in prayer. Even though I still had hearing loss in the natural realm, I could hear well in the spirit realm. I prayed that God would give me "elephant ears" in the spirit. My appreciation for the voice within grew. Though I did not get healing from hearing loss, I found something better: spiritual gold. I realized that gaining the spiritual hearing came directly from spending so much time praying for the restoration of my natural hearing. Desperation had motivated me like nothing else ever had.

In 1984, it had been seventeen years since I left home. I had read through my Bible many times. I knew that the Bible says a person receives power when the Holy Spirit comes upon them. Church teachings indicated that speaking in tongues was evidence of this power. I wanted this power—which some called prayer language, praying in the Spirit, spirit language, or heavenly language—because I thought it would help me get healed.

I had first heard people speak in tongues when I was sixteen at the little country church. Because I did not know how to pray that way, I felt spiritually inferior and excluded from the love circle between God and certain believers. I reasoned that others were better than I or had a closer relationship with God than I did. The pastor said praying in tongues was a spiritual gift, and people should not ask for gifts. He and his wife said they could only pray in tongues when they were moved by the Holy Spirit. From that description, I thought the Holy Spirit somehow took over, and then people could pray in tongues. I wanted to be close to God, so I waited and hoped that God would approve of me and I would be able to receive a prayer language.

One evening after my workday ended, I checked into a hotel and began my usual prayer routine. That night I wondered, was I the one blocking myself from praying in tongues? Did I need to do something? I thought perhaps I should try speaking some sounds. I knelt by my bed and tried to say "words" without engaging my English language. It was awkward and did not feel right. The words came from my mind, not the Holy Spirit. Immediately I heard a gentle, kind voice within say, *Do not mimic my Spirit*. I was relieved and stopped trying to make something happen. I knew what I had tried was not authentic. I apologized. I wanted the real deal, and that was not it.

3

Healing Miracles

Bit by bit, my new inner guidance was leading me away from the pastor at the country church where the fear corral began for me. In 1984 I started attending Bible Temple, a charismatic church in Portland, Oregon, where Reverend Dick Iverson was leading a congregation of around two thousand people. In my new church environment under Pastor Iverson, I realized interpretation of scripture varied within each church. So began my metamorphosis and emerging from the fearful, self-debasing cocoon I had lived in for so long.

I found reasons to believe that God was not mad at me, and my destiny was not limited to a life of religious slavery. I began to allow myself to feel my humanity rather than believe that I was supposed to die to myself. I was relieved that this church was not like the first I had attended. It did not condemn close fellowship with relatives and family members who were not "born again." Pastor Iverson said, "If you do not love and minister to your own families, who will?" This was a relief to me because I wanted very much to rebuild the broken relationship with my family.

A couple of years later, Dr. Larry Lea, author of the best-selling book *Could You Not Tarry One Hour?*, was traveling the country holding prayer clinics. Following Dr. Lea's method, Pastor Iverson began teaching us how to use the Lord's Prayer as a guide to spend an hour in prayer every day. He emphasized the importance of spending quality time this way, telling us,

"Something miraculous happens when you pray an hour a day." Inspired and motivated, I began the practice of praying for one hour a day, guided by an outline from Dr. Lea's book.

My relationship with the spirit realm grew, and I experienced the richness of life that follows quality time spent in prayer. I did not know it yet, but multiple things were synchronizing like a puzzle coming together; events were lining up to bring needed changes and blessings into my life. The first was Pastor Iverson's sermons and instructions, and the second was a small book educating me about prayer language. The third event was the Healing Miracles Crusade.

In 1987, twenty years after I first heard my pastor speaking in tongues, I was still waiting to receive a prayer language. Someone gave me a little book that explained how to receive the gift of tongues (prayer language). Reading the book changed my perspective, as it said that praying in tongues is a process of yielding to the Spirit, which some refer to as the Holy Spirit. My part was to release the words using my voice. Thoughts and spoken words in any language are creative energy. The prayer language is an avenue Spirit can use to create an outcome that benefits all. When a person allows the Holy Spirit to flow through them via a prayer language, they are yielding to and joining forces with the creative, loving life force of the universe. Only good will come from words spoken by Spirit.

Although I now understood prayer language differently, I still did not know how to do it. That is, until the Healing Miracles Crusade. Advertisements announced that Charles and Frances Hunter, well-known healing evangelists, were coming to Portland, Oregon, to host the crusade. Healing miracles manifested wherever the Hunters ministered, so I was eager to attend. I needed a miracle to restore my hearing to normal. The Hunters held two days of preparatory meetings before the main crusade. Christians could attend the prep sessions, so I went to immerse myself in as much spiritual energy as I could.

On the first day, I entered the meeting room early, and many chairs were still empty. As I sat down, I became aware of a young woman sitting alone in my row about twenty feet to my right, crying with no one to comfort her. The chairs between us were vacant, and as compassion filled me, the thought came to me, You go comfort her. As I sat down by her side, she responded with gratitude and shared that she had come to the meeting to be healed of damage from a car wreck that had twisted her skeleton and made walking difficult. She walked in front of me to demonstrate. I watched her right foot arch out to the right and then swing back in as she planted her foot on the floor. She could not walk without her foot turning outward, and she had a pronounced limp. I found these words coming out of my mouth: "God is going to take care of you." We talked a bit more, and I returned to my original chair and sat down.

As the meeting began, I realized I had misunderstood its purpose. The Hunters were training this group to pray for the sick during the crusade. These people were apprentices learning the methods that activated miraculous healings. They had prepared themselves in advance by reading a training book provided by the Hunters. I felt a bit awkward. I would not have come if I had known it was a training meeting. I had no intention of praying for others during the crusade; I did not consider myself qualified because I had not been able to heal myself.

Charles Hunter told us he had had remarkable success in helping people pray in tongues. He said he would lead us all in prayer, and everyone who wanted to pray in tongues was to join in. He explained, "You do not have to be religious about it or kneel or stand in a specific prayer-like position. You ask God to give you the Holy Spirit and trust that he will. I want everyone to place their hand on the back of someone next to you. Let us join together as one. Release the words that come to you, use your vocal cords, keep your eyes open, look up to God, and smile. Now open your mouth, use your voice, and trust God to pray through you in a heavenly language."

We were all connected by hands touching backs. He led in his prayer language, and the entire group of about four hundred people started praying out loud. Unknown words formed in my spirit; I opened my mouth, released my vocal cords, and my long-awaited prayer language flowed out. It was my voice, gentle and quiet, but I was speaking a foreign language with words I didn't recognize. It was effortless and fluent, like breathing, like an ocean wave, like a bird flying across the sky. Such joy, such refreshment!

After the meeting ended, I sang in my new prayer language almost the entire way home. I noted that it came from the area of my heart, not from my mind. It required no effort, no thought; it just flowed.

✻

I am grateful I learned to release my prayer language in such a delightful setting. The experience was without religious postures or ceremonies. It was authentic, comforting, enlightening, and lasting. From then on, I used my prayer language as often as I could. When my native language of English feels limiting, I use my prayer language to release the emotions of my heart. In private, I use my prayer language to pray for others. When I use my prayer language in this way, it is with the intention of supporting others with the energy of love. I am allowing myself to be a conduit of Spirit, which works for the highest good of all.

I feel a warm energy flow over and in my body when the Spirit is moving in me. It is subtle, recognizable, and authentic. In my experience, this is my cue that Spirit is initiating prayer or communication. Prayer is communication, and it is two-way; listening is the receiving part. Over time, I have learned to ask for an interpretation of the message coming through my prayer language. Sometimes I receive an answer; sometimes I do not. I have learned that if I need to know, I will be told.

I always respect the initiation of Spirit and release my prayer language. I don't have to understand the words or what Spirit is accomplishing (creating). I become a conduit for the energy of love; I have learned to trust. I know that language creates, words create, and the prayer language of Spirit is no exception. It is the law of our universe that thoughts and words precipitate all manifestation. I trust Spirit is always up to something good. As I focus on breathing evenly and quieting my mind during meditation, I sometimes release my prayer language on each exhale. Allowing the prayer language to flow in this way is similar to using a mantra. It is gentle and soothing, and requires no thought; thus, it helps bring about the desired quietness of body and mind.

�֍

After my joy-filled experience during the first training meeting, I returned to attend the second meeting. This time the Hunters asked individuals within the group to come forward if they needed healing. They demonstrated how to pray for others. It was radically different from the format I had learned in my church. The Hunters assumed a position of authority and made direct commands to the body, such as "Spine straighten and come into perfect alignment, in the name of Jesus." I saw people straighten up and be healed right before my eyes. I watched goiters shrink and legs appear to grow out as heels came into perfect alignment. It was glorious, being an eyewitness to miracles.

Then Charles Hunter stopped calling people forward. He looked out over the crowd and spoke: "There are too many people here for Francis and me to lay hands on. You are believers; you know what to do now. The Spirit is present among us to heal. If you need healing, lay your hand on the back of someone near you and have them pray for you."

I felt a hand on my back and realized someone wanted me to pray for them. My mind was racing. "Oh no! I am not prepared or qualified to pray for a healing miracle for someone else." I turned around and looked straight into the eyes of the young woman I had spoken to the previous day—the same woman I had told, "God is going to take care of you." I thought, "In a crowd of four hundred people, how can it be that she was directly behind me? How is this happening?!"

I sought for words, wanting to explain that I could not help her. "I have not read the Hunters' book; I did not realize this was a training meeting."

She calmly looked me in the eye and dismissed my concerns. "I have."

I saw her faith and her desire for me to pray for her. I also saw the desperate look in her eyes and decided to quit talking, knowing I could destroy her hope and faith if I said any more. The Hunters had demonstrated how we were to speak to the body; I knew she needed her skeleton to come into alignment. I had seen miracles, and Charles had said we were operating under their spiritual umbrella.

I reasoned I could pray for her, I could copy the Hunters' format that I had witnessed. She stood up, and we started at her neck level and worked down. "Spine come into alignment, arms come into alignment." The new method of speech felt awkward. I was not asking God to heal her body; I was commanding her body to align. She coached me, explaining which parts of her body needed to be aligned. Then she sat in a chair, extended her feet, and I held her heels in the palms of my hands. There was well over an inch difference in the length of her legs. I spoke to her legs, "Legs become even, in Jesus' name." Nothing happened.

Charles had told us not to quit instructing the body, not to give up. I kept praying, "Legs become even in Jesus' name. Leg grow out in Jesus' name." Over and over, I repeated the command using as many creative ways as possible to keep saying the same thing. I directed all my energy and focused my eyes and thoughts on her legs. Then I saw movement; the shorter leg was inching forward on my palm. I looked up at her and said, "It's moving." I continued holding her feet until the heels were evenly aligned. It was a glorious, victorious moment for both of us.

It was time to leave; the meeting had ended. I had missed my opportunity to be prayed for because I had spent my time praying for the woman. The next day the Miracle Healing Crusade would be open to the public. I wanted my hearing restored, and I planned to attend.

I arrived at the coliseum and found a place to sit. Though the crowd was large, once again, the woman I had prayed for found me. She was radiant as she told me what had taken place after we parted the day before. During the night, her body had completely healed. Her skeleton was now totally aligned. Her right foot no longer arched out; she had a normal gait and no limp. We rejoiced together in her healing.

The team of helpers lined up on the coliseum floor, ready to pray for those who desired to be healed. The helpers were standing side by side in two long lines that faced each other. The two lines of helpers created a winding pathway for those who wanted to be prayed for. The helpers would raise their hand whenever they were available to pray for the next person needing prayer. Those who wanted healing entered the human pathway and stood in front of anyone with an upraised hand.

I lined up with others and walked the pathway. A young couple in the line had their hands raised, indicating they were free to pray for someone. I stopped in front of them and explained that I needed healing from hearing loss. I could not help but notice the fear in the young girl's eyes; she was so nervous her eyeballs appeared to be vibrating. I remembered how I had felt the day before when the woman had asked me to pray for her. As I looked into this young woman's jiggling eyeballs, I felt my hope and confidence slipping away. They prayed, and I continued down the human pathway and out of the column.

It was so noisy in the coliseum I was not sure if anything had changed with my hearing. I went to the women's restroom, where it was quiet. It seemed to me there was no change. By the next day, I knew my hearing loss had not changed.

My mother knew I had gone to the healing crusade. She called me the next day and asked, "Well, did you hear the birds singing this morning?"

"No, there is no change in my hearing. I need to keep in faith."

My hearing had not changed, but I had. I had received my prayer language and had been a conduit in a healing miracle for another. Life was good.

SPIRIT VISITATION

My prayer language became more fluent as time passed. I could be in my garden thinking of planting flowers and simultaneously allow my prayer language to flow out. For me, it was as easy as breathing, and it was comforting, like someone putting their arms around me and helping me. In time, I began to experience what I call Spirit visitation.

Spirit visitation came when it chose to. There was no switch to turn it on; it was like the wind, moving wherever it desired to move. I could quickly identify Spirit visitation because I physically felt it. Gentle energy would wash over the crown of my head, over my shoulders, arms, and body. I often felt tingling energy in my left hand. Sometimes it made my heart tender, almost like sadness, and gentle tears came to my eyes. It became a signal to me, a call to stop, pray, and listen. This awareness might come while I was doing housework or when I was meditating or praying.

When I felt Spirit's presence, I responded with respect. I would bow my head and allow my prayer language to flow out until the energy lifted. Sometimes the flow of prayer language was a strong current like water rushing over a dam, and other times it was like a gentle stream. Physically it felt like loving energy coming out of my heart center; the prayer language flowed effortlessly, totally bypassing the mind. I always welcomed the warm waterfall of Spirit energy. It was pure love, and sometimes a message came with it.

Spirit energy would sometimes come and help me when I was distraught or at a perplexing roadblock in life. I would use my prayer language to release the pent-up emotions. Other times I would be feeling just fine, and Spirit visitation would unexpectedly come. I learned the unexpected visits often contained a message for me. I would pause when the energy stopped flowing and ask, "What?"

The answer would come in a form similar to but different from thoughts of the mind. Some call this the still, small voice. Typically three words came into my mind. Using my journal, I would write down those first three words, and then the rest of the message would keep flowing into my mind. I just took dictation as it came. Countless times I have received direction, comfort, and love from these messages of wisdom and guidance.

I developed a deep appreciation for these wise interjections in my life. I could not initiate them; they always came when Spirit chose to bring them. The messages were always perfect in timing and conveyed perfect love, wisdom, and guidance when I needed it most. I wrote every message in my journals. Using my prayer language, asking questions, and recording the answers became integral to my relationship with Spirit.

BEGINNING OF VISIONS

I continued the practice of praying for an hour each day and using my new prayer language. During my prayer times, I began asking for wisdom, revelation, and prophecy. My spiritual life expanded when I received my first message from Spirit accompanied by an inner vision that gave me a peek into my future.

At that time, I was in my tenth year of working as a district manager for JoAnn Fabrics. A new regional manager was in charge of the district managers on the West Coast. She was young and intent on climbing the ladder of success, and her methods of dealing with people seemed harsh and unfair to me. Working under her direction took the joy right out of my job because I was obligated to do what she required. She used the district managers like a broom to sweep away any store managers she thought were hindering her quest for success.

During my prayer time, I knelt down on my knees and began asking for help. I said, "God, this woman—What am I supposed to do?"

There was no waiting to hear; the voice within answered before I finished, *Honor her.*

My mind jumped to the Bible scripture, "Honor those that have the rule over you." I was surprised by this directive, but I trusted the love and wisdom that spoke to me. This love always knew the right thing to do in every situation. I was under the jurisdiction of the regional manager and it was my job to honor her. I responded, "OK, God, I can do this."

When I went back to work, I had to face store managers who were in upheaval about the attitude and demands of the new regional manager. I was deeply aware that they were going to take their cue from me. I carefully phrased my statements and guarded my attitude. "She is the boss. This is how she wants us to do things, and we need to honor that." They adopted my attitude and cooperated with the new demands. They had no clue that I also found the regional manager's methods distasteful. I honored her because I knew it was the right thing to do.

I continued to work in this uncomfortable environment, but the job had lost all joy for me. In private, my prayer life was evolving into a delight. When Pastor Iverson had taught about praying for an hour a day, he had said, "First prayer is a duty, then a discipline, then a delight." I found that to be true for me. The ability to hear the wise, loving counsel of Spirit was meeting a deep need in me. I developed the habit of quietly waiting after I prayed. I would listen for anything that Spirit might want to say to me. One day I had finished praying and was listening. Within my Spirit, I heard what the Bible refers to as the still, small voice.

I set before you an open door.

I contemplated this a moment. Curiosity set in, and then in a spark of boldness, I asked, "What is the door?"

Turn this way.

I instinctively knew that I was to physically turn and face north. I remained in a kneeling position and turned my body north. My eyes remained shut, and then clearly in my mind, I saw a blackboard. Written in large letters on the blackboard was the word *school*. I was thirty-seven years old at the time. I knew what kind of school it was because it had always been in my heart. I wanted to get professional training and use my artistic skills. Then I heard more.

And I will send the money.

I thought that statement was odd because I was earning adequate money to go back to college and did not know why I would need more. That was the end of the dialog. I had received a message and seen a vision. Now I needed to wait and find out where it would lead.

※

Nine months passed. It was the end of the work week, a Friday in August. I was checking inventories and procedure compliance in one of the stores under my supervision. I leaned over a fabric bin and suddenly heard the clarion voice of Spirit from within.

Quit your job.

I was startled. My back straightened up, and a big smile overtook my face. I knew that trusted voice well. "Really? No problem!" My mind summed up my situation. I had money in savings. I knew this was my opening to go to school. I could get a part-time job and move forward in life. I had the weekend ahead of me, and when Monday arrived, I called my regional manager with my prepared speech.

"I am calling to give my two-week notice."

"May I ask why?"

I had anticipated that she would ask that question. I knew better than to tell her she was the reason I wanted to leave the job. Furthermore, I was in no way going to share my conversations with Spirit. I responded with the carefully crafted response I had decided on during the weekend. "I just don't feel that I am the right person for this job anymore."

She paused a moment and then revealed, "You need to know that last Friday, corporate headquarters called a meeting of the regional managers. They are cutting payroll, and ten district managers were selected to be laid off. You were not on that list. You have been a good district manager. I am going to award you the severance pay that would have been given to you if we had laid you off."

My mind flashed backward through the chain of events that were now connecting like dominos falling in a line. Spirit had told me to quit my job the same day corporate had held the meeting to cut staff. Before that, Spirit had told me, *Honor her*. Minor shock waves of awareness brought clarity to my understanding. Had I not obeyed Spirit's voice and honored her, she would no doubt have let me go without giving me the severance pay. Spirit had told me, *I will send the money.*

The timing was right, as fall semester was about to begin. I immediately enrolled at Mount Hood Community College. A staff member told me the graphic design classes I wanted were already full. I knew I was supposed to be in those classes. I asked, "What do I need to do to get into the classes?" The staff member said, "The only way is by getting a signature from the course overseer." She gave me his office location.

The old Diana would have just accepted defeat, but this new Diana had been told by Spirit that she belonged in that class. I gathered every scrap of artwork and design work I had done over the years and went to the overseer. He looked over my work and said, "If you can do this well without any training, you deserve to be in the class." He signed my ticket to be enrolled. I was in!

The severance money was vital in making it easy for me to focus on getting my degree in graphic design. I was able to be a full-time student without having financial concerns. I rented a room directly across the street from campus in the home of a single mom with a sweet little girl. My living situation was pleasant and the location was ideal, as I could stroll past trees and over the manicured grounds to reach my classes.

I worked hard and maintained a 4.0 GPA, which earned me free tuition and scholarships each semester. As icing on the cake, my calligraphy teacher asked me to be her apprentice. She was in charge of the college print shop, and each year she chose one student to work with her. I loved this apprenticeship; the job provided extra money and graphic design experience as well.

※

Everything was perfect except my hearing. I continued to pray for healing from hearing loss and also began the process of getting hearing aids. The warning that I might go deaf loomed in my memory. I chose graphic design thinking it would enable me to earn a living even if I lost my hearing completely.

I could not hear the instructors, so I went to Sears and got a square amplifier designed to fit over a landline phone. I sat in the front row of all classes and held the amplifier next to my ear. Holding the amplifier and taking notes was difficult, so I transitioned to using a tape recorder at every class and then transcribing afterward. This method helped me get straight *A*s. I never missed a word, and I could review every detail from each class before a test.

One day I decided to go all out and fast as well as pray for my miracle healing, something I had learned to do in church. I fasted for three days until I reached my limit. I had heard nothing from Spirit and was discouraged. Walking into my bathroom to brush my teeth, I looked into the mirror and saw the sadness and disappointment in my eyes. I wanted to forget about praying for healing. I was tired of obsessing, seeking, praying, and crying about my hearing loss.

I wished I had never heard about divine healing; it had caused me years of grief, always hoping I would get healed and then being disappointed. I reasoned that if I had not known that God could heal, I would have worked at accepting my handicap years ago. All these years of praying, tears, feeling rejected, and now three days of fasting and no result. I leaned forward over the sink to brush my teeth and said with resignation, "OK, God, if you want me to be deaf, I will be deaf."

Immediately I heard the kind, loving voice within. *It is not my will for you to be deaf.*

I was overjoyed. I did not get what I had prayed for, but I was free from the fear of going deaf. After that, my hearing stabilized and quit declining. I did get hearing aids and found they were not so bad, and other people were unaware I even wore them. I stopped putting so much effort into being healed and went on with my life.

My Treasury of Love

4

Desires of the Heart

My entire world had changed in nearly every area in 1987. Besides finding my prayer language and a new church, leaving a ten-year job to pursue a degree and career in graphic design, and living in a new place, I got news that my first pastor, who was in his eighties, had died. I wept in relief that this man I had feared was gone, and I prayed, "God, please don't ever separate me from my family again." His teachings and assertions that he was God's anointed prophet had convinced me to alienate myself from my family, forgo college, and disregard the advances of young men who had shown interest in dating me.

In the transition from JoAnn Fabrics to college, I lost all the daily, familiar relationships with those I had worked with. I was relatively new at Bible Temple and did not know many people. I was trying to humbly reestablish a relationship with my mother and with my brothers, who rightfully still held grievances against me regarding my departure from the family. My college classes were filled with students in their early twenties, and I was in an entirely different stage of life. In the twenty years since my encounter with religion in high school, I had never dated. I was thirty-seven years old and felt very alone.

One day the stress of all the changes in my life and the lack of close friends and family surfaced in an unexpected way. I was in my psychology class, a course required to obtain my degree. The professor was teaching about our need for various types of relationships. Because my life had been almost entirely emptied of relationships, the topic triggered something deep inside me. When the class ended, I walked out the classroom door, aware that I was experiencing a stress reaction of some kind. Something within demanded my attention; suppressed emotion overcame me and produced an inner trembling that compelled me to stop walking.

I leaned against the hallway wall and felt my abdomen shaking my petite frame. I pondered this new experience as I focused on composing myself. I was grateful there were no witnesses around, so I did not have to explain my trauma to anyone. My intuition informed me that this trembling was a deep longing for companionship, love, and friends. Teachings in my new church had kindled self-worth, and self-worth kindled a desire for companionship. I could feel the enormous loneliness in my heart, and this time I was not shutting it out.

I hurried back to my room, which was a short walk across the campus grounds. The internal shaking continued, and I wondered if I was having some type of nervous breakdown. I had never had emotions physically shake my body like that before. I got on my knees by my bed, released my prayer language, and let it flow until all the pent-up emotions subsided. From experience with my prayer language, I knew something significant was happening. This type of emotional outpouring was a download, a prayer that was coming through me. It was not coming from my mind; it was flowing out of my heart.

I prayed, "Father, I need someone to love, and I need someone who will love me."

That type of prayer was not typical of me since I usually did not request things for myself. I reflected on some recent divorces I had witnessed and knew that my life with Spirit would never end. It could not; it was who I am. I needed someone who was spiritually compatible. I added another request to my prayer: "I want someone who loves you as much as I do."

It was the kind of unbridled prayer that gushes forth from the depths of the heart. My experience told me that this prayer was divinely birthed. Something would come from this.

DIVINE WINKS AND CLUES

After releasing my request, I went back to life as usual and waited to see what would evolve. One day the single mom I rented my room from asked me if I would like to go to a movie with her. I thought it would be fun, so off we went. The movie revolved around the phenomenon of people falling in love during the time of the full moon. I enjoyed the film, and because I rarely went to the theater, the theme stood out in my mind. This movie would take on greater significance for me as my life unfolded. Spirit likes to bless us with surprises and will often arrange clues and hints about good things to come, and I later came to see this movie as a divine wink.

My romance antennae were up, and I opened my heart to allow myself to look around at who was eligible in my church. I went to events organized for single adults. I remember standing in church and hearing the deep male voices in the pews behind me. That deep male sound comforted me; I longed for the balance of male and female to become a reality in my life. Because I had been raised with four brothers, I knew how to relate to men and was comfortable with the way they processed life. I loved the way they could simplify and stay on course; I enjoyed their strength and their stories. When I was a young girl and we had family reunions, I loved to sit by my dad when all the men gathered to talk about hunting and fishing and to laugh at the jokes they played on one another during campouts.

I continued my college classes and was enjoying a course in learning to play racquetball. As I walked across campus to my room, I sent up a prayer asking God to send someone to play racquetball with me. I thought that some girl would come along in answer to that request.

At the time, I was working in the print shop for my calligraphy teacher. She had a happy, sunny personality, and her radio was always on, broadcasting uplifting music and current events. One day she announced that her daughter had just had a baby and had named him Tom. She asked me what I thought of the name. After a moment of reflection, I responded, "I never met a Tom I did not like." She laughed and laughed and kept repeating the phrase over and over. "I never met a Tom I did not like. I never met a Tom I did not like."

It turned out to be another divine wink. When my work in the print shop was over for the day, I headed back home. When I entered my bedroom, I saw the message indicator light blinking on my phone. The message was from a man named Tom whom I had only recently met. On the recording, he asked me if I would play racquetball with him. I knew who he was, barely. I did not know his last name yet. He was new to my church, and we had seen each other there on a few occasions. At a church picnic recently, he had been near me in the food line as I mentioned to some people I was chatting with that I was learning racquetball in a college class.

The phone message caught me by surprise. I did want someone to play racquetball with, but I was thinking of a girl, someone more on my skill level. I remembered Tom; he was tall, handsome, and quick to smile. He was the personification of a car salesman, a very nice one. I had been watching him play ball games with some of the other men. He had an athletic body and had made his sweatshirt into a fashion statement by cutting the neckline into a deep V shape, revealing his attractive hairy chest. He had cut the sleeves off at bicep level, and his arms were tanned and muscular. He wore cut-off shorts above the knee. His hair was dark, medium length, and nicely permed into soft curls.

I was a bit nervous about playing racquetball with a man who was quite athletic. I was still a novice and had been playing for only one term. However, I had prayed for someone to play with, and here he was asking if I wanted to play.

I called him back and said, "Yes, I want to play racquetball."

So Tom and I met a few days later to play racquetball. He was indeed very athletic, and I did my best to keep up and hit the ball. Blisters were forming inside my shoes, but I said nothing to him of my discomfort. I was having fun, and he was kind enough to let me hit the ball occasionally. After the game was over, we sat down to talk in the lounge area. I listened as he poured out things that were on his heart. I watched him run his fingers through the curls of his dark brown hair. Maybe he was a bit nervous, but I was delighted that he was sharing his life stories with me.

He then informed me that he had tried to find a guy to play racquetball with him but had been unsuccessful and remembered during the church picnic I had mentioned that I was learning racquetball. He said he was a bit nervous about asking me to play and was relieved to be able to leave his request on my telephone recording. He then added, "I don't want you to think this is a date."

Whoa! I was shocked that he would say such a thing. I said nothing, but mentally I thought, What a jerk, what a terrible thing to say. I am not the type to chase after a man. After all, I had deliberately sidestepped every invitation I had received in the past thirty-eight years. All because I did not think it was *God's will.*

I had had no preconceived ideas about our meeting. I had accepted the invitation because I wanted to play racquetball. He had invited me because he wanted to play racquetball. That was all there was to it. I was a little miffed at his remark but kept that reflection to myself. I had had a good time. We parted ways.

※

Back home after the racquetball game, I walked into the kitchen. As I opened the doors under the sink to toss something in the garbage, I heard the unmistakable voice of Spirit.

This is the one.

I stood bolt upright and began mentally digesting what I had just heard. I smiled and said, "Wow, he is a good one."

Suddenly I was on a different mental track when I thought of Tom. I went to my bedroom and fell asleep. I woke in the middle of the night, and the full moon (like in the movie I had just seen) was shining through my window, its light filling my room. I felt the warm energy of Spirit flowing down over my head and shoulders and recognized that a message was forthcoming. I took out my paper and pen and began to write what I heard.

The message I received spoke of the future as though Tom and I were already married. I was told there would be some difficulties at first, but they would resolve over time. This forewarning enabled me to handle the difficulties that surfaced later on.

Tom called me the next day and asked me to go to the fair with him. I felt like a flower bud ready to burst into bloom with the new information Spirit had given me regarding him. He arrived in a white pickup truck and opened the passenger door for me. Trying to be prim and proper, I sat in the truck seat as close to the passenger door as possible. He grinned and said, "What are you doing way over there?" I laughed and quickly scooted across the seat, and snuggled right next to him. It felt like we had known each other forever, even though we were on our second day of getting to know each other. When we arrived at the fairgrounds, he reached over and took my hand and continued to hold it as we walked and observed the booths. I very much enjoyed his touch, and when we got on the rides, we sat as close to each other as each ride would allow.

Then came the moment of truth. As we walked the fairgrounds holding hands, each of us silently enveloped in our own thoughts, Tom stopped and looked at me. He asked, "Has the Lord been talking to you?" I felt like I would fall into the earth as my mind raced to know how to answer him. Here was a man I barely knew, and yet I knew I would marry him. The first mental realization was, "I can't tell him the things that I have heard from Spirit, not now." I also knew that I was not able to hide the truth. My countenance had always been like an open book. To avoid the question and deviate from facts would be written on my face, and I knew it. So I chose my words truthfully but carefully. "Yes, but I can't tell you what right now."

Tom invited me to go to lunch with him the next day. We sat opposite each other with our hands joined in the center of the table. Before lunch ended, we both shared what had happened to us after that first racquetball game two days ago. He had said it was just a game, not a date. However, both of us were praying and watching for a special someone, and our two hearts had drawn us together. Tom had also heard from Spirit just like I had. As he was driving home after the racquetball game, he heard an inner voice urging him to ask the question, *Is she the one?* He succumbed to the inner voice and asked, "Okay, is she the one?" In response he heard, *Yes*.

Well, it was out on the table now. We both knew that the other felt the same magnetic energy, the same push. The next day, day four of our acquaintance, Tom came over to my home carrying a slender red satin ribbon. He asked me to hold out my hand, and as I did, he tied the ribbon on my ring finger. He said that he was led to enter a fabric store and buy the ribbon. He then went on to tell me all the things that needed to be put in order. "We will need to get furniture and a place to live." He continued to explain all the things that we would need to have a home together. I said nothing; I just listened and watched this man thinking, planning, and organizing our future. His take-charge attitude was charming and delightfully masculine to me. He left and went back to his apartment. That night, I got a phone call from Tom. He said sheepishly, "You didn't answer me." He was referring to his plans about marriage.

I responded, "You didn't ask me, and I don't want to hear it over the phone."

Tom picked up the cue. Seven days after our first racquetball game, he invited me to come to the home where he rented a room from an older woman. He led me to the back patio as a full moon flooded the night sky, prompting me to remember once again the movie I had recently seen. He knelt on one knee, looked into my eyes, and asked me to marry him. Of course, I said yes!! We then kissed for the first time. All of these synchronized, enchanting events had transpired in one week.

Next, Tom invited me to walk with him along the shore of the Columbia River. He was concerned about earlier events in his life and felt a need to disclose things in his past that he thought I should know. He watched my face as though trying to read my thoughts and then offered, "I don't want to have any skeletons in the closet."

As I had been forewarned by Spirit that there would be some rough times ahead, nothing Tom said caused me any concern. Tom had become a new person and had made a commitment to serve Christ, but he still had debt and past issues he needed to resolve. We were engaged that summer and honored the request of our church leadership to at least wait one year before marrying.

Before Tom and I met, both of us had been praying that God would bring that special one into our life. We were both grateful for the events that brought us together. As we sat in church during that first week after we were engaged, I looked down at Tom's hand holding mine and remembered a favorite scripture, "Take delight in the Lord, and he will give you the desires of your heart." I had been given the desires of my heart.

✤

During our year-long engagement, Tom worked at preparing for our future. I worked at finishing my final year in college and getting my degree in graphic design. I continued to maintain straight *A*s, and each term I was awarded a free tuition scholarship. Both years I was selected to work in the print shop as the apprentice. The second year in the print shop was different because now I was wearing my engagement ring. That ring sparkled, my eyes sparkled, my heart sparkled, and for me, the whole world sparkled. I held up my hand and showed the engagement ring to my boss, Marty. She smiled and said, "Good things just seem to happen to you, don't they?" It was true, and working for her was one of those beautiful gifts that Spirit had arranged for me.

One day Tom came by to see where I worked. He stood in the office doorway and placed both his hands on the door jams. He was so handsome and I was so proud of him, I looked his way and beamed a smile. Not quite sure if he should walk in, he just stood there looking my way and watching for cues from me. Marty immediately got the connection and said, "So this is Mr. Wonderful!" The name stuck. Mr. Wonderful became my pet name for Tom. It appeared on my Christmas and anniversary cards to him, and later in a song I wrote about him.

At the end of the term, Marty gave us our final assignment in the calligraphy class I was taking from her. We were to use the new calligraphy skills we had learned and create art of our choosing. I chose the words I had spoken before meeting and falling in love with Tom, "I never met a Tom I did not like." I embellished the first letter with gold ink and artfully arranged the remaining words on my paper; in the lower right corner, I included a black-and-white tomcat in the design.

Marty knew the significance of that phrase. She had met my Tom and knew how much I loved him. She had seen me through several transitions, first as a student struggling with hearing loss, then adjusting to hearing aids, and now a bride-to-be. She was happy for me. I got an *A* on the calligraphy assignment and framed the art. It became my first Christmas gift to Tom before we married.

※

LOVE SONG

I graduated in June and married Mr. Wonderful one week after graduation on June 10, 1989. My wedding was one of the happiest days of my life. As I entered the aisle wearing my bridal gown, my eyes met Tom's as he waited for me by the altar. He had beautiful blue eyes, and they were happy and full of love for me. That was the look I had seen in my father's eyes when he looked at my mother. It was a look that I cherished and was deeply grateful to have found. Many times during our marriage, I would recall the depth of Tom's blue eyes looking at me, waiting for me to walk down the aisle and become his wife. It was the first time in my life I felt unconditional love from another person.

On our tenth anniversary, I gifted Tom with a song of love that recalled the time I had prayed, asking God to send someone to love. Over the years, if I went too long without singing it, he would ask me to sing it to him again. Tom had lived in Texas before we met, and he had a slight drawl that I thought was charming. His pet name for me was Baby Doll. I reference those unique traits in the song I wrote for him.

10th Anniversary Love Song to Tom Brown
by Diana Brown, June 1999

I prayed for someone to love and God sent you my way.
I prayed for someone who'd care and God sent you.
I thank him every day for the special way he made you,
Mr. Wonderful, I love you.
I like being your "baby doll,"
I like the way you say that name
with your slightly southern drawl,
And when you smile at me in your special way,
Mr. Wonderful, you make my day!

※

Tom was easy to live with, a humorous, happy man who had the persona of Santa Claus. He was a salesman and had attended Zig Ziglar seminars and practiced the principles Zig taught. I heard him quote more than once, "You can get everything in life you want if you will just help enough other people get what they want." Tom liked to make others laugh, and with his quick wit and warm smile, he could do just that. He was a man who would knuckle ruffle the hair of a young boy and cause him to grin from ear to ear. Tom always kept his old Army bag stuffed full of baseballs, bats, mitts, and sportswear in case an occasion arose to play sports with the boys.

He was a helper, a hero, a protector to the underdogs in life. He had served in the Army for five years and been one of the youngest to be promoted to sergeant; he had served in the Honor Guard. He was generous and wanted to please. I quickly learned not to mention too many things that I liked or wanted, especially if they were expensive or beyond our financial resources. Tom would move earth and sky to obtain whatever I wanted. He worked at maintaining a sunny attitude. One time he said, "If God never did one more thing for us, he has done enough already for us to be grateful for the rest of our lives."

Before he met me, Tom had spent many successful years selling cars, motor homes, and insurance. He had worked his way up from car salesman to finance manager, working on a commission basis. He told me he did not want to go back into the car business. He had terrible memories of the business; it was evident how much he loathed that line of work. He desired to follow the integrity Jesus had modeled, and the tactics Tom had previously learned as a car salesman conflicted with his new value system. He told me some of the incidents he had seen during his years as a car salesman. One salesman had gotten angry at a customer who was not yielding to his high-pressure tactics and threw the customer's car keys on top of the car lot roof. When Tom decided to get out of car sales, he prayed, "God, please don't put me back in the car business."

He worked a variety of jobs, mostly involving sales, but he deliberately sidestepped commission-based car sales jobs. There was a time when he was between jobs and putting pressure on himself to be a provider. He spoke openly to me, wondering if he should go back into car sales. I responded, "God does not expect you to do something you hate. Don't do it; something will open up." He did find the next place to work, and it was not selling cars.

Tom excelled wherever he worked. He was self-motivated, always early to arrive at his place of work, and diligent. He would work hard and earn any bonus that was offered. He rarely had a sick day, and if he did come in contact with something going around, he just kept smiling and moving as if he were not affected. I wondered if it was his happy heart that protected him from succumbing to the flu. I openly admired him and continually affirmed him.

One time Tom said to me, "I wish I could see myself the way you see me." Underneath his smiling persona was a wound from childhood. His father had never praised him for his accomplishments. Tom always felt like no matter what he achieved, it was never good enough. When he was in Boy Scouts and told his father he had advanced in rank, his father merely said, "How come you are not an Eagle Scout?" When Tom very quickly advanced to the rank of sergeant in the Army, his father said, "Why aren't you a colonel?"

And so it was that Tom always felt the pressure of "not good enough." The words from his father weighed on him.

5

Dark Night of the Soul

The deep need to advance and to be more caused Tom to search for his unique purpose, the thing that would be "good enough" to spend his life doing. The church often spoke about finding one's purpose in life. He read a book about George Mueller and the orphanages he built. The book planted a seed in Tom's heart, and he told me he would like to do work like George Mueller had done. I replied, "Where are the children that need homes? Times have changed; there are no orphans on the streets." We then discovered that in the United States, there are places called children's homes where overwhelmed single parents did indeed place their children. Tom thought that starting and running a children's home was something he could do.

Tom's quest for fulfillment led him to accept an invitation from a pastor friend. His friend also had a dream and desire to make a difference in this world. His friend had grown up in Montana, and he and his wife wanted to return to Kalispell to start a church there. We were having dinner together when his friend popped the question to Tom. "Will you come to Montana with us and help start a church?"

Without asking me what I thought and without a moment's hesitation, Tom said yes. He was working for a corporation that allowed him to work from home. His job was mobile, and his boss was supportive of Tom's dream to start a children's home. Tom was ready for change, ready for action, and thought maybe his destiny would unfold in Montana. The laws in Montana were more flexible, and Tom hoped he could open a children's home there. I was a bit shocked that Tom had committed himself without discussing it with me. Regardless, I was accustomed and molded to being a follower and raised to be a submissive wife who honored her husband. I loved Tom with every fiber of my being, and he was my hero.

We moved to Montana.

※

The Flathead Valley seemed to be at least ten years behind the civilization we had left in Vancouver, Washington. There were no major shopping malls, and many streets had no speed limit signs. Wildlife was abundant. Sightings of bear, moose, deer, elk, geese, eagle, and osprey were frequent. Before moving to the Flathead Valley, I had seen a painting of Native Americans on horseback crossing the waters of Flathead Lake. It depicted a fuchsia pink sky reflecting in the lake. I assumed the artist had embellished the scene and that the colors were artistic license. I thought nothing in nature could be that pink, but I discovered that my assumption was wrong. I saw for myself the fuchsia pink sky and its mirror reflection in Flathead Lake.

The lakes in and around Glacier National Park had a color palette unique to the area. I saw pools of water and rocks that nature had painted in turquoise, mauve, vivid pink, and soft grays. The park was less than an hour's drive from our home, and it was a favorite place for us to go. The panoramic views along the fifty miles of Going to the Sun Road revealed glacial lakes and jagged peaks covered with snow. Going to the Sun crosses the continental divide, and that knowledge brings a feeling of exhilaration, like sitting on top of the world. Breathtaking forests, glaciers, and abundant wildlife are calming to the heart. It was not uncommon to see deer, black bears, and mountain goats.

Tom and I worked alongside the pastor and his wife to help them start a new church. The church plant was soon doing well, and the pastor and his wife had a small, stable, growing congregation. We also spent many hours walking over beautiful properties, searching for a location for a children's home. Tom's research led him to discover Cal Farley's Boys Ranch in Texas. We felt free to take a break from Montana and get some firsthand experience of how to run a children's ranch, so we applied for work at Boys Ranch as house parents. We were immediately accepted, and off we went.

It didn't take us long to realize that our concept of running a children's home was nothing like the reality we experienced at Cal Farley's. Our initial enchantment with the ranch rapidly led to disillusionment in multiple ways. The closest town was sixty miles away, so we had no relief from the ranch environment day after day. Our shifts as rotating house parents began to take a toll on us. We worked six days in one home with thirteen boys, then had three days off. On our next shift of six days, we went to a different house with a new group of thirteen boys. During our days off, we stayed in an on-campus apartment provided for house parents. With its cold concrete floors and uncomfortable beds, it did not feel like home but drained our energy and enthusiasm. Our health began to suffer from eating cafeteria-style meals that catered to the desires of the children, with many deep-fried entrees and very little fresh fruit.

We did not fit in with the environment but continued doing the best we could. Each day was like a large grinding wheel, wearing us down. I felt like my life was slowly leaving me; I felt dead inside with no desire to face the day. I felt no energy or sense of wellness. Three times in six months, we both got sick. We were exhausted, taking antibiotics, and our three days off were spent struggling with illness.

Tom was first to recognize that we were going under spiritually, physically, and emotionally, and he called a halt to us working there. He summed it up nicely: "We need to go home."

PRECIOUS CHILDREN

We returned to Montana and to our church friends. We both found jobs, and then he and I opened up a topic we had discussed before. Tom and I had met late in life. I was thirty-nine and he was forty when we married. His two sons by an earlier marriage were adults. Deep within my heart was a desire for a daughter, a passion that did not go away. We began discussions about adopting a little girl. We had been licensed foster parents when we were in Oregon, and we soon became foster-adopt parents through the Department of Human Services (DHS) in Montana. In the foster-adopt program, foster parents have first consideration if the foster child assigned to their home becomes adoptable. We were making ourselves available for a miracle.

Being a foster parent in this type of program is an emotional roller coaster. The children that come into your care are precious and so lovable. You have to be careful or your heart can easily get broken. We had no way of knowing which children might become available for adoption.

Because we wanted to adopt, DHS placed the youngest children with us. The first child placed in our care had been born seven weeks early, so he was tiny and fragile. I was a stay-at-home mom, and it was my first experience caring for a premature infant. The warm softness of his skin next to my face felt like a touch of heaven to me. I felt so blessed while caring for him. I had a sling-pouch that wrapped over my shoulder so I could watch him at all times. He lay quietly in the pouch directly over my heart. Little David grew strong, and then DHS decided his permanent placement would be with his grandparents. I felt the loss of his sweet presence and realized that I could not allow myself to attach or I would suffer. I resolved to give the children the love they needed but guard my heart so I could release them when it was time for them to move on. I assumed the mental stance of being a drop of love in a little person's life for as long as they were in my care.

Soon after that, two brothers became our foster children. They had the same mother but different fathers. The younger brother was six weeks old. After the brothers had been with us a few weeks, DHS called us to see if we would take another foster child. We waited in anticipation in the office. A caseworker rounded the corner, holding the hand of a sweet little girl. The girl's face revealed that she was worried, and an air of sadness hung over her. Britney was eighteen months old, with blond hair and blue eyes. I was aware that she resembled me and prayed within my heart, "God, don't take this one away." After a few weeks in our home, this darling girl emerged from the dark cloud that hung over her. She became radiant, joyful, and full of life in the safety of our home. I could only imagine what sorrows she was leaving behind.

One day as I sat on the floor with the three children, Britney inched her way closer to me and climbed into my lap. I felt overwhelming love for her, and the bond of mother and daughter began. I adored her mannerisms. Her grasp of language was advanced for her age; she would walk into the kitchen, hold up her cup, and make her request. "Ice." She loved ice.

As time moved along, DHS placed two more boys in our home, so we had five precious children under the age of six, four boys and one girl. To my delight, Britney became a ward of the state, and within six months, we were able to adopt her. For ten years, I had been praying for a daughter, so adoption day was a time of great celebration.

DHS planned to place three of the four foster boys with relatives. The two brothers that had different fathers were going to be separated. Brock, the youngest of the two brothers, remained with us. His older brother was placed with his birth father. Sadly, while baby Brock was in our care, his birth father took his own life. I went to his crib and prayed over him that he would not suffer as a result of his family link to a very troubled man. His mother did not adhere to the requirements of DHS, and Brock continued in our care for two and a half years.

Brock's mother indicated that she would like us to adopt him. Tom and little Brock had a sweet relationship; it was delightful to watch them both light up with joyful smiles when they saw each other. The years of being together had formed a bond, and we had emotionally transitioned into Brock's parents, not his foster parents. All of our hearts were knit together. Brock became a ward of the state and was available for adoption. My husband and I had been his foster parents the entire time and were first in line to adopt him.

※

As we waited for Brock's case to progress, one of the caseworkers asked us if we would take in another foster child. She was nine years old and in a special therapy treatment because she was a pathological liar. Her previous foster parents had lost their license due to stories she had told caseworkers about them. My husband and I had developed a good track record, and the caseworker asked if we would take her in.

It is sad but true that if a child makes allegations, DHS removes the children from the foster home. They do this to protect themselves and the foster children. The foster parents have no rights or protection if a child makes an accusation. They lose their license as foster parents and become victims of the children they were trying to help. Some children recognize the power they have to manipulate the system but are too young to realize the devastating and far-reaching effects of their accusations. The young girl they wanted to place in our home had already learned she could influence the DHS system.

My Christian background and the teachings about loving everyone overruled the misgivings I had about this new foster girl. Tom was very discerning and pointed out to me that she did not seem to fit into our family. It was only a short time before she told a lie about us. We told the caseworkers the truth, but to no avail. They informed us we would lose our license and the foster children would be removed from our home. The nine-year-old girl who had started this landslide of events had settled in with us and was doing well. She cried when she found out DHS was going to put her in another home. She tried to undo what she had done and asked the caseworkers to change their decision, but it was too late.

The caseworkers had recently come under criticism because they had not handled an incident in another foster home properly. They were being heavy handed and overreacting in our case to make up for their past error. My husband saw through their harsh, unreasonable actions and told them, "You are using us as an example, as a warning, as a spectacle, a sample of your might. You are hoping to put fear in other foster parents. You are trying to vindicate the mistake you made in the other home."

What he said was true, but we were the perfect out for them to regain face.

We were brokenhearted at the thought of losing Brock. After raising him for two and a half years and hearing his mother tell us that she wanted us to adopt him, we had given our hearts away to him. Brock and Tom had a tight bond. I would watch their happy faces when Tom would get on the riding lawn mower and put Brock on his lap. Round and round they would go, smiling, laughing, and so happy to be together.

We pled with the caseworkers to be reasonable, but they were like iron gates. In our last meeting, we had to leave Brock with them. Even at his tender young age, he knew something was deeply wrong. At the end of the meeting, as they took him away from us, he cried out, "Don't leave me, don't leave me!!!" He knew we were being ripped apart. The emotional tearing broke all of our hearts. Highly intuitive for a child, Britney recognized that it was a wrong action on the part of the adults and exclaimed to me, "Brock belongs with us!"

"I know, baby, I know."

We went to our friends, the pastor and his wife. I watched my husband weep in the arms of his friend. I had never seen Tom break down like that before. He was always the courageous one, the hero, the sunshine, the joy, the laughter. Seeing his broken heart and hearing the echoes of Brock's cries tore my own heart into shreds.

※

In the following weeks, I had nightmares and could hear Brock's pleading cries. My grief and my anger at the callousness and stupidity of the caseworkers kept me from sleeping. I would rise in the middle of the night trying to escape my volcano of emotions by releasing my prayer language. I would leave our bedroom and go into a room farthest from the bedrooms where my husband and daughter slept. My cries were loud as I used my prayer language to express the emotions of my soul, and I tried to muffle them with a pillow. I pled and used every technique I had heard that described how to get what you want from God. At that time, many churches were teaching about using your authority in Christ, claiming what you want.

There was a dark cloud of emotion over me. The joy was gone, and my spirit was broken. I knew when I prayed there was no energy helping me. I was fighting an unyielding force of some kind. I was not flowing with the stream; I was fighting against a current. I knew I did not have victory; I could feel it when I was praying. I fought anyway; I could not understand or submit to this horrible event. Why?!? We were not guilty; we loved the child; he loved us. It was not fair or just.

I read the scriptures that told the story of King Herod killing all the Hebrew babies. I related to the grief, and I understood the agony of those families. Brock had come to us at six weeks old; he had a skull fracture from being struck by caretakers. We wanted him; we loved him; he was happy with us. No one else was there for him; we were his parents in our eyes and his eyes. When I prayed to God, I would cry, "He is *my* baby. Please, God, we love Brock." The bond between us had formed; he *was* my baby. He cried out, we cried out, "Give us justice!" But no justice came.

It never occurred to me that there might be a larger plan than mine. I assumed I was supposed to fight that darkness with all my strength, and it was exhausting me. I was miserable. Looking back, I now know that I was fighting against a plan beyond my ability to understand. While I was fighting for justice, I never prayed a prayer of submission; I never said, "Not my will but yours be done." It did not cross my mind that I should submit myself to these events that I could not control. I was in the midst of a generation of church teaching that was jokingly referred to as "name it and claim it." I knew we had done nothing wrong and DHS had made a mistake. I assumed if I prayed and fought for our rights, justice would prevail, and DHS would give Brock back to us.

This experience of government injustice was a first for me. For the first time in my life, I understood what it felt like to be wrongfully dishonored and shamed. I had lived my entire life endeavoring to be a person of integrity. I had never had anyone think I was lying. It just was not who I am. To have a child removed from our home and our integrity questioned was so disgraceful. The experience hit home the reality that bad things do happen to good people. I told Tom, "If this can happen to us, it can happen to anybody." Above that pain was the horrific loss of the child, the nightmare flashbacks of Tom's tears and Brock's cries. I wanted to fix it so badly, and I could do nothing. I loved Brock, and I loved Tom. My heart would break over and over at the memory of their tears and seeing their pain.

I was very angry with the caseworkers' lack of grace, love, and professional handling of our case. It was the first time I had ever felt hatred in my life. I knew that if I did not rid myself of the anger, it would consume me. I had to drive by the DHS office on the road from my home to the grocery store. Seeing the building would bring up the sorrow, pain, and anger inside me. I tried to look in the opposite direction when I drove by. I wanted peace, so I began to work on my heart to replace anger with forgiveness. I forgave them verbally; I willed to forgive, believing that eventually, my heart would follow. I prayed that they would come to realize their error and not cause more suffering to others.

It took a lot of effort and many prayers, but my anger finally subsided.

※

We had the right to request a hearing, so we got an attorney and made our appeal. Every time our opportunity for a hearing came up, DHS would cancel and reschedule. They always found some excuse not to come to the hearing. Our attorney warned us, "No one wins against the state. They are canceling because no one will take their case. They don't have a case; they are embarrassed." Each time DHS rescheduled the hearing, it cost us more money; they were stalling and financially bleeding us dry. We spent $10,000 retaining an attorney for two years and finally had to stop. We realized they could continue to evade a hearing forever. We were getting deeper in debt, and DHS had moved Brock into another state.

I tried everything. I wrote to the governor explaining our dilemma. He responded that he was sorry, but there was no support system for foster parents. I went online looking for a support system for foster parents. Online, I found a host of other foster parents who had received the same horrible treatment we had. I read story after story written by people who had opened their homes to foster children and had become victims of an abusive system. The foster parent stories were heartbreaking, and I realized it was futile; there was no help for foster parents, no justice for them. Foster parents were a disposable commodity.

What the caseworkers did, and how they did it, was wrong in every way and left a devastating mark on our hearts. I can only imagine what little Brock went through. He was torn from a loving home and never allowed to see us again. The caseworkers said if they allowed visitation, it would be too hard on him. We were all in love with each other, and the pain would make matters worse. I asked that they give us the same opportunity they gave to birth parents. Birth parents were put on probation and had to pass all state requirements to get their children back. I reminded the caseworker that they were not following their own rules regarding doing everything they could to cause the least disruption for the child. They declined, knowing full well we would pass every test. They were more interested in trying to save face.

Four long years later, the state reviewed our case, and we were vindicated. We received a letter from our attorney. The state had sent a written acknowledgment that we had done nothing wrong and should never have lost our license. Our attorney stated in his letter to us, "It appears that you were wronged by the State."

It was too late. Brock was gone, and we did not know where he was. We had heard that he was somewhere in the Midwest. We realized it would be unwise to pursue him because we would be in danger of devastating him again by tearing his new world apart. We did not know if he would even remember us, he was so young when they took him. So for his sake, we let the matter rest.

✤

Brock was the second loved one I had lost in my life. The pain was unrelenting and kept surfacing over a period of five years, just as it had after my father's death. I would see a photo or a person who resembled them, I would say their name or someone else would mention their name, and the grief would surface. It would rush up to my lungs, heart, and throat, and the tears would gush out. I simply did not know what to do with the grief. It never really left, just simmered below the surface until triggered by a memory or an incident in life.

Still, I learned many things from that loss. For one thing, I learned what it felt like to be fighting against what is. There is a knowing when you are laboring in vain, and your prayers bounce back like a ball ricocheting from a brick wall. When the energy does not flow, when the force is against you, it is then that you must take time to reevaluate. If you realize that you are laboring against mighty forces, take heed. Some things need to be; they are part of a bigger plan for the greater good of all.

I have heard that when you pray for things that are in alignment with the greater good, the entire force of the universe is with you. When you align with the universe, the words that form your prayer will flow out easily, like riding a bike downhill with the wind at your back. In stark contrast, when you are asking for things that are not in alignment, you are working against the wisdom and energy of the universe. In those cases, you are struggling to pedal the bike up the hill. These energetic signals are a cue and kindness beyond comprehension.

We can't see the entire picture of our life and all the lives connected to ours. During times we don't understand, we can trust the integrity and love of Spirit. I have learned when there is no energy, no Spirit igniting my prayer request, there is a good reason. Einstein's famous quote addresses this issue. "The most important decision we make is whether we believe we live in a friendly or hostile universe." I believe we live in a friendly universe, where there is a perfect plan for each life, and our life touches other lives in an ongoing domino effect.

✣

When we first moved to the Flathead Valley in Montana, we were told that the Native Americans called it the Valley of Tears. We entered the valley so full of faith, expectation, and joy. We loved the wildlife and beautiful Glacier National Park. We thought we would finish our days in Montana. Now we could not bear to stay there any longer. It had become a valley of tears for us.

After more than a year of resisting and striving for justice, we realized we would not get Brock back. We had been in Montana for seven years. I told Tom that I wanted to go back home where the rest of our family was. We were broken in heart and spirit. Our faith was wounded, our dreams and plans shattered. We wanted away from that place, away from the memories. We met with our friends, the pastor and his wife, and told them of our plans to go home. Tom's two sons from his first marriage were thriving in a local church back in Washington. We knew their church pastor; he had been a part of our church roots. We wanted to be with our family, grandchildren, and old friends. We packed up our dear little adopted daughter and headed back home.

    I eventually became grateful that sorrow had forced us to return home to Washington. We would never have left Montana if all had gone according to our plans and dreams. There was yet another plan that we did not foresee.

6

Words from a Prophet

In December 2003, Tom, Britney, and I were back in Vancouver, Washington, trying to pick up the threads of our lives and heal from our loss. Both Tom and I knew we had to move beyond disappointment and the negative emotions of grief and anger. We resumed attendance at our former church. The pastor saw us sitting in the congregation and spoke to us in the hearing of all. He said, "Tom and Diana, I have a word for you. You did not fail; you were just in training."

※

About six months after we moved back to Vancouver, our church held an evening service with a guest speaker. The speaker was recognized as a prophet who had a spiritual ability known as "word of knowledge." I went to the evening service by myself because Tom had to work a night shift on his job. Usually, Tom and I sat in the front rows. That evening I just wanted to hide out in the back of the crowd and listen.

After the congregation had finished singing worship songs, the prophet began choosing individuals from the crowd of people. He would point them out and ask them to join him on the stage. Then he would share the message he had received from God for them. The entire congregation watched and listened as he spoke to each individual.

Over my many years in church, I had come to trust these types of gatherings. I had seen the spiritual gifts and word of knowledge in use many times. A head pastor is cautious about who is allowed into church to minister to the congregation in this way. The prophets don't know the people they are ministering to and are dependent on their spiritual hearing to relay the specific message that Spirit has for each person. I had known many people who had been encouraged and guided by prophetic messages of this nature.

This particular evening, the guest prophet gave words of knowledge to several people, and then he left the stage and began walking down the center aisle. He came nearer to where I was sitting. He explained to the congregation how he prepared himself before services. He would pray, and while in prayer, through his gift of spiritual sight, he could see which people he was to give a message to. When he walked down the aisle, he looked for the face he had seen during his prayer time. He stopped at the end of the row where I was sitting and motioned for someone to come to him. I then realized he was looking at me. He said to me, "Have I spoken to you yet?"

I replied, "No." He indicated for me to come. I walked with him to the front of the church and up to the platform.

It had been only six months since Tom and I had given up the futile battle to get Brock back. The shock and emotional pain from defeat, retreat, and losing him were still very much a part of my life. It had been two years since DHS had taken Brock from our life, and I was still struggling, trying to free myself from the pain. I still prayed for Brock's welfare, trying to be his spiritual mother protecting him. I had no way of knowing if he was in a nurturing, loving home. In my heart, he was my son, torn from my life. Losing him had brought out the same emotions I had experienced when my father died. I did not know how to deal with the loss of someone I loved. That was my state of mind on this night during this special service.

As I stood on the platform facing the prophet, he had his eyes closed and said out loud to himself, "This is beautiful." He was referring to the message he was receiving from Spirit. Then he began to tell me what he was receiving.

"Your heart is so heavy, and it shouldn't be because God's going to do what He told you He would do. You know…" (he paused, eyes closed, listening, and then resumed) "…this is awesome." He knelt down in front of me, holding my hand, and began to sing this prophetic song:

> *I see every tear you've cried*
> *And I hear all of your secret prayers you pray to Me.*
> *And I am here for you, says The Lord, to answer you.*
> *Oh, I'll not leave the family this way*
> *I am going to answer your cry*
> *I'm going to wipe every tear from your eye*
> *   and show you that I am faithful.*
> *I'm a God who sees, I'm a God who hears*
> *Every breath my people pray*
> *You'll rejoice at my goodness*
> *You'll rejoice at the beauty of my hand*
> *I have heard you and I'm here for you*
> *I have heard you and tonight things are turning in your favor,*
> *   in your favor.*

The song ended and the prophet continued with these words:

> *For nothing has been destroyed, nothing has been lost that I am not able to give back says the Lord, and you have asked yourself, "Why?" And you have asked yourself, "Why? How much more, how much longer is this going to go this way?"*

> *God says, "Daughter, just yet a little while and you will see the goodness of my hand. And you will see that I am a God that does not leave one fragmented piece undone, but I am able to put all the broken pieces back together again because I am a master artist." And God says, "Even as you love art and poetry you will have a new song. And you will have a new poem and out of that poem will come deliverance for many other women that have gone through the loss that you have suffered and the things that you have dealt with that you have been too ashamed to share."*

> *God says, "Through your writings will come forth healing for others. So this night I touch you." And the Lord says, "I breathe a fresh*

breath of my Spirit..." (he swept the air with his hand)...*there it is* (he spoke reverently)...*my God! "...a fresh breath of my Spirit upon every area of your life and nothing, nothing is too hard for the Lord."*

After delivering the message to me he ended with these words: "Father, I release your word upon her life right now and I give you the glory for the testimony that will come forth."

The words he spoke to me brought up deep emotion. I could not refrain from tears as I stood weeping and absorbing the reality that God was acknowledging my brokenness. All of my prayers and pleading trying to get Brock back, days and hours of painful emotions, painful events, and the dark night of the soul had led up to this moment. A total stranger had just told me that God saw my tears, heard all my prayers, and was for me.

I was perplexed that Tom had not been able to come because of his work. I knew he needed encouragement also.

I have been an artist all my life. Art has always been part of who I am. In the second grade, I was the one who painted Santa and his reindeer on the windows as we decorated for Christmas. I sold paintings; I painted backdrops for church plays. When God sent me to college, it was art once again, in the form of a degree in graphic design. I had heard many prophetic words spoken over other people, but I had never heard art mentioned. I had heard many people receive calls to various types of ministry, but I had never heard art called a ministry.

That God took the time to acknowledge my love of art and that my art would benefit others was a surprise to me. The reference to my writing was another surprise. I did not consider myself to be a writer and had never aspired to be one. I had never thought that any poem, song, or writing of mine was of any significance to God. In fact, as I write these words right now, it has been sixteen years since that prophet spoke those words into my life. This book is the first time I have written for the benefit of others. This book does contain poems and songs that came to me over these past sixteen years. Yes, it is indeed my desire that what the prophet spoke will become a reality. He said, "Through your writings will come forth healing for others."

That is the reason I am sharing my story. I want to be of use; I desire the events of my life to be of help to someone else. If what I share helps another person's heart heal, every event and experience I have had will have been worth it.

※

We wanted more contact with Tom's two sons (my stepsons) and his grandchildren, so we talked to the pastor of the church we had been attending and explained that we would like to switch to their church. He graciously understood. We had past connections with their pastor; he had been a youth pastor at Bible Temple, where Tom and I had met, married, and served. While we were in Montana, that youth pastor had become the head pastor of Tom's sons' church in Vancouver. Joining this church was a natural and easy transition because we knew many of the people in the congregation. The bonus for us was getting to see our family each week.

Tom and I served as house church leaders during midweek Bible studies that met in host homes. We made some new friends and felt secure in the integrity of the minister. The pastor had excellent administrative skills, the people were friendly, and it was a very supportive environment.

Our young daughter eventually found her niche as a Sunday School teacher's aid. Britney was blossoming and her creative gifts in art and music were expanding. She had grown taller, slim like a willow, and had an enchanting wit. She also delighted everyone with her lovely singing voice and was chosen to sing a solo at a Christmas play. Her voice resonated with depth of soul, and during one rehearsal parents stood and applauded after she sang her part.

Britney did not like to talk about being adopted; she wanted to blend in and be like other kids to stay in her comfort zone. We both had light brown hair and blue eyes. People who assumed Britney was my biological daughter sometimes commented, "You sure can tell you two are mother and daughter."

We would look at each other and grin, our hearts affirming, Yes, we are! Tom totally won her heart; she lit up whenever she saw him, and they would go on outings together to satisfy their sweet tooth. When we first adopted her, she had no trust in men and little trust in any adult. Tom was a father she could trust. He would sit in his recliner and she would curl up in his lap while he held her in his arms. She was adventurous and had a boldness that I admired, being able to speak her convictions without fearing what others might think.

✤

In February 2006, three years after Tom, Britney, and I returned to Vancouver, we decided to quit renting and get back into homeownership. Housing prices were soaring; we purchased a 1,090-square-foot house on a quarter acre of land with the idea of renovating it and then moving into a larger home. We worked side by side, doing all the work ourselves. We upgraded and repaired, added flower beds and a garden. We replaced all the interior doors, painted the fireplace and walls, added laminate flooring, and installed new bathroom fixtures. I used my artistic abilities to add custom murals, faux stone designs, and borders on walls. To make the narrow doorway between the living room and kitchen seem wider, I painted Romanesque pillars on each side. To adorn the pillars, I painted green ivy vines swirling their way to the top. After entering our front door, one person exclaimed, "I feel like Alice in Wonderland."

Then in 2008, the housing market fell, leaving many homeowners caught in upside-down mortgages. The equity in our home vanished in one day. Tom had been in real estate sales at one time and was disturbed by this change in events. He was talking about getting out of the home by entering a short sell agreement with the lender. I just listened, not knowing what to do. I had always depended on Tom's knowledge regarding buying a house, moving, and selling. I was a total follower in that regard. He always found homes for us that were pleasant and comfortable; I never needed to concern myself with thinking about housing.

During the economic recession, businesses were closing and men were without work. Then Tom lost his job as well. For an entire year, he searched for work. He tried everywhere to find employment. Meanwhile, we stayed in the little house.

✤

GIFTS OF LOVE

The plus side of that year of unemployment was that Tom and I got to spend a lot of time together. We would take drives into the country. I would take photos and return home to paint scenes of wildlife. Tom was encouraging me to get back into painting pictures. I had, for the most part, given up painting when we got married. I had used my artistic abilities only to help enhance church plays and decor. While we were in Montana, I had been feeling nudges to paint again. The wildlife and beautiful landscapes called out to the artist in me. I started a series of wildlife paintings and always found joy whenever I was painting.

In February 2009, Tom asked me to come into our home office. His tone was solemn, and I could tell he had been in deep thought. He knew me well and knew how conservative I was regarding voicing my desires. He knew that I would rather be without than put us under financial strain. Yet he wanted so very much to give me things and to bless me. He said, "You could have gone very far in art if you had not married me."

I assured him that he meant far more to me than anything I might have accomplished by pursuing a career in fine art. I had spent my years doing what I wanted to do most, and that was being with him and helping him. He showed me a website of an art school in Scottsdale, Arizona. "I think you should apply for this scholarship they offer."

"Tom, if I got the scholarship, how would we pay for the flight and lodging?"

"We will find a way."

I filled out the application, and to my surprise and joy, I got the scholarship. The scholarship awarded me one week with a professional artist of my choice. I looked over the list of instructors and chose professional painter Donald Demers. I was ecstatic; I had not felt that kind of excitement since the day I was married. I loved art, and I loved creating. I was on a high from anticipation.

In April 2009, the week to enjoy my scholarship arrived. I went to

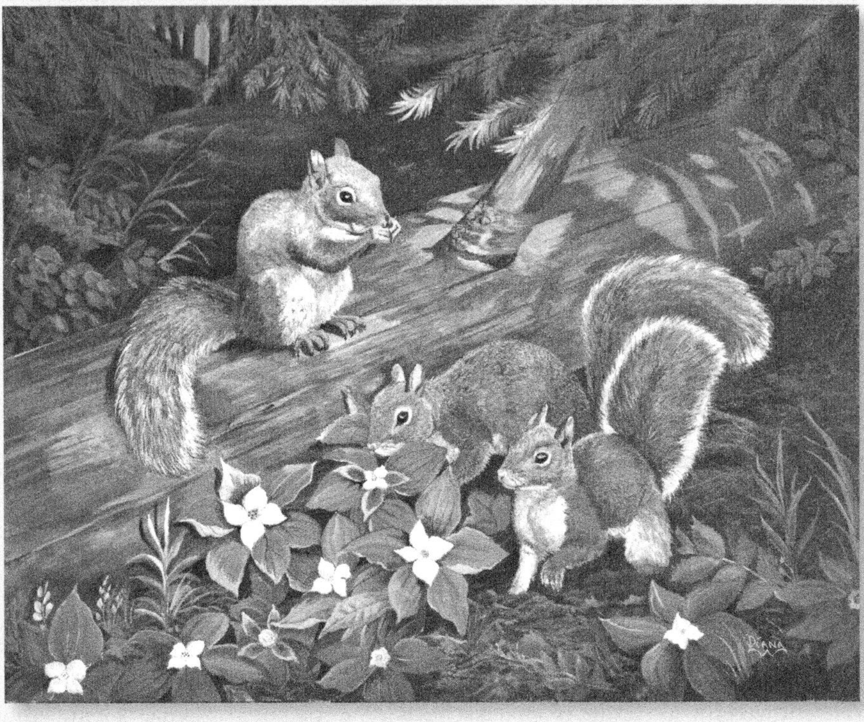

Scottsdale Artist School and spent the week with other students studying under Donald Demers. I was intimidated and yet eager to learn. Studying art with a professional artist was like a dream reawakening within me. I learned a great deal about painting outdoors on location. When I returned home, Tom would take me out on the forest trails that followed the local rivers. I would set up my gear and paint, and he would fish.

June 10 would be our twentieth anniversary, and as our special day approached, both of us were thinking about what gift we could give to the other. Tom had a small thirteen-foot aluminum fishing boat that he loved and pampered. He had built a nice boat seat and painted it turquoise. The boat was resting under a canvas tent in our side yard. I approached Tom with a request. "Will you pick out a fish-finder that I can buy for you to put on your boat? I want to get it as an anniversary gift."

He smiled and responded, slowly savoring the words, "A fish-finder." He accommodated me and selected a fish-finder for himself. Then he once again called me into the home office and showed me that he had found online some special equipment for artists to use while painting outdoors. He had selected the set he wanted to buy for me. It was a portable hinged paint box with an attached easel. The box had a tripod and also an umbrella that could be attached to shield the artist from the hot sun. Of course, such a collection of goodies was exciting to me. Tom looked me in the eye and, knowing my tendency to say, "No, we shouldn't spend the money for that," he said, "Please, let me buy it for you." I agreed, and both of us were happy to give and receive those gifts that we wanted.

To celebrate Father's Day, I told Tom he could choose anything he wanted to do for the day, and Britney and I would accompany him. He decided to go fishing on the lake and use his new fish-finder. The three of us spent an entire day out on the lake. After the first four hours in the small boat, I was feeling mild motion sickness. Not wanting to spoil his fun, I did not mention it. Tom caught six fish, and Britney and I were fascinated watching the fish show up on the fish-finder screen. You really could see them swimming below the boat! That night when I went to bed and closed my eyes, I could still feel the boat's rocking motion on the water.

It had been almost a year since Tom lost his job. He was nervous because unemployment compensation was running out. I suggested that he choose a place he would like to work and volunteer his services. Maybe something would open up, and in the meantime, it might make him feel better. He volunteered to work at a framing shop. The process of getting dressed up and going to work each day did bring him some joy. He continued to fill out many online job applications and check the mail for responses. He wanted to provide for his family and applied for food stamps just in case. I offered to find work, but he wanted me to be a stay-at-home mom. He felt it was important that nine-year-old Britney always be able to come home to a parent. He said, "God can provide through me."

With the unemployment checks coming to an end, Tom made a decision based on desperation. He reached back into his work history and knowledge of car sales. Selling cars at a dealership was a straight commission job, but it was a chance to make money. He was to start on Monday the following week. I knew he had bad memories about working in car sales and hoped it would only be temporary and something else would open up for him. I remembered his prayer from years ago, "God, please don't put me back in the car business."

He wanted to go camping for the weekend before he started on Monday. On the night before the camping trip, I came home from my monthly meeting at the Portland Fine Art Guild where I was a member. Our living room light was off, and moonlight streamed through the front window. Tom was reclining in his white leather chair, looking out the window at the moon. The moonlight was soft and inviting. There was a quietness and a peace that beckoned me to stay with him for a while. I knew he had been praying; the past year had been challenging for him. Seeking employment with no success had taken a heavy toll on Tom's typically sunny and upbeat personality. He was facing reentry into straight commission car sales, a job he loathed. He rarely talked about his distress, but I knew his heart was heavy with questions and disappointment.

I wanted to spend that moment with him, so I laid aside the things I brought home from my meeting, grabbed a pillow to kneel on, and placed it next to his chair. I draped my arm over his midriff and lay my right cheek on his tummy. He gently put his arm on my back and cradled my right shoulder with his hand. I turned my face toward the window to see the moon, my chin still resting on his tummy. The soft moonlight flooded my face, and Tom said, "What are those shiny eyes thinking about?" It was a quiet, precious moment between two people who loved each other. We were facing life together, not knowing what would come next, just being.

✺

As I woke early the next day, July 7, 2009, Tom's hand reached over and clutched mine in a loving gesture. The grasp said, I am glad you are with me; I am relieved I am not going through this alone. Tom got up first and began packing for our camping trip. I drifted off to sleep again. A little later, Tom came in and lay crosswise on our bed, his head near my right side. I reached over and put my arm around his neck, cradling his head with my hand. I noticed a heaviness in his spirit that was not typical of him. He said to me, "Why didn't you say something when I told you I was going back into the car business? You usually tell me not to do things I don't want to do."

I responded, "You were so discouraged; I felt that taking that job would not block God from bringing you a job you liked. I thought it would encourage you and act as a filler to occupy your time until the right job comes along."

I got out of bed so I could help get us ready for our trip. We had reservations at a campground and were looking forward to some family play before Tom started his new job. I looked out our living room window and saw Tom packing our truck. I went into the kitchen and began gathering the food I had prepared. I packed the potato salad into a container and placed it in the cooler along with our other camping food.

While we packed, nine-year-old Britney rode her bike around the neighborhood. She had come back into the house, and then suddenly, she was by my side in the kitchen. She said, "Daddy is on the floor." I followed her into the office and saw Tom's twisted torso lying there as if he had fallen while trying to turn around in his swivel office chair. My first thought was that he was playing a joke. Tom was always teasing and making others laugh. I then saw his broken glasses near his cheek. I placed my hand across his mouth; there was no breath. I felt his pulse, and there was none.

He looked so uncomfortable in that twisted position. I wanted to do CPR but could not move his heavy six-foot-three frame. The phone was directly in front of me, and I dialed 911. I informed the operator of the location and situation. She shouted, "Man down!" and I could hear the sound of sirens coming. I knelt beside Tom and remembered all the stories I had read about people who had had near-death experiences. I tried to focus, to be calm. I felt so ill-equipped to know what to do. I leaned over his body and placed my cheek against his way-too-quiet chest. I was stunned and in shock.

I tried to pray, remembering the stories about others who had prayed loved ones back to life. I searched within myself for the flow of Spirit energy to help me. I needed a miracle, and yet it seemed impossible to request one; I was frightened. I continued to try to voice my requests in prayer. Deep within my heart, I heard a soft, familiar voice gently say, *No*.

The world around me became a blur of activity. I was unprepared for the events unfolding before me. There were sirens, ambulances, fire trucks, and paramedics arriving at my house. As I watched in a daze, the paramedics went into the office and began using all their techniques to revive Tom. One neighbor said to me, "He's going to be OK." I wanted to believe that, but inside I thought, You do not know that; you are just trying to be comforting.

In what seemed like a flash, the paramedics came out to me and said, "We have done all we know to do; he is gone." The men began to leave my home, eyes looking down, quiet steps, heads bowed. One of the paramedics attended my church, and he stepped aside to tell me that it appeared to be cardiac arrest. Tom's heart had just quit beating.

✣

My stepson and daughter-in-law arrived. They told me they would like to take Britney home with them so I could attend to the details. Britney was in distress. Trying to hold on to her father in some way, she picked up his watch to claim as her own. She looked me in the eye and exclaimed, "We are not going to have any more fun. It is too soon!"

I don't know how many people had made phone calls, but somehow my world had been alerted that Tom had died. My home was full of people, some that I knew and some that I did not know. I stood in our hallway and tried to answer questions and comprehend all the information given to me. My pastor was there, and he asked me if I wanted to spend some time with Tom before they took his body. I went into the office, shut the door, and wept on Tom's chest. I said to him, "Well, sweetheart, you don't have to go back into the car business; you are free."

People were asking what they could do. I asked one to cancel our reservation at the campground and another to take down the tent we had set up in the backyard. Some people from my church told me they would arrange for meals and visitors to come to my home. I tried quietly to object because it was my nature not to trouble others with things I could do myself. They told me I needed to let them help, and so I agreed. I was so grateful that others had taken charge. Some already knew what I had not experienced. My whole world had just changed, and I would be changing.

People began leaving my home; some took Tom's body to the funeral home. A friend asked me to choose the clothing Tom would wear. I decided on his herringbone black-and-white blazer; he always looked so handsome in that. I returned to the living room and saw the empty chair where Tom and I had shared some precious time together just the night before. My mother sat quietly on the couch. My friend was carrying Tom's blazer out the door, taking it to the funeral home. As I watched her, I spoke to myself in soft, quiet words, "I don't want this to be happening."

I sat on the couch, stunned by the rapid chain of events. My husband had died; my daughter had gone to stay with my son and daughter-in-law; my life as I knew it had just ended. My mother and I sat alone in silence in my living room.

I could not sleep that night; a constant parade of memory images flowed behind my closed eyelids. I could see Tom on the floor, his body jumping from shock as the paramedics tried to restart his heart. My mother was sleeping next to me in the big king-size bed. I got up and went into the kitchen, trying to find some solace; in reality, I was trying to find Tom. I noticed a small framed picture of our family of three sitting on the kitchen countertop. Britney must have placed it there for me; she was always so thoughtful. I picked up the image and held it to my heart, somehow trying to extract Tom from that image. The emotional pain inside me seemed unbearable and inconsolable.

Later, as members of my church came to my home bringing evening meals, I realized how wise that gift was. The visitors brought some momentary comfort as they shared stories and helped me. One woman said to me, "You are not alone." When she spoke those words, she was touching on an issue I had faced all my life. Before marriage, I had always felt very alone. I remembered my father looking at my mother with love in his eyes. I had wanted a love relationship like that. Tom had given that to me. Now he was gone, and I wanted very much to *feel* that I was not alone. The loss of a beloved husband had torn a massive hole in me. My journey of change had begun; the experience of being a widow lay before me. I did not know any of the answers to my questions.

7

Shaken to the Core

The first year after Tom passed, I cried every day, mostly in private so I would not upset my daughter. The constant flow of tears concerned me; I wanted to stop the grief for the sake of my darling Britney. In despair, I would get in the car and drive, hoping no human on earth could hear me. I would call out Tom's name at the top of my lungs, though I knew there would be no answer. I so desperately wanted to hear his voice. My cell phone became a symbol of his departure. I looked at it and tried to absorb the reality that he would never call again. The tears would gush out if I mentioned his name, and I wondered what the sorrow would do to my health. I did not want to bring illness onto myself as a result of painful emotions.

At times I would reach out and touch a photo of him, or his personal belongings, trying to connect with him. He loved to fish, and the Christmas before he died, I had given him a soft, warm flannel shirt with fish patterns. I put that shirt in my closet and often slipped it on at night to find comfort in the memory of his nearness.

I held my sobbing daughter in my arms many times during those months following Tom's death. I heard her crying one night and went into her bedroom. With a heart-wrenching cry, she sobbed, "I want him back." I held her close, rocking her slender frame, and could only affirm, "I do too, I do too." There was nothing I could do to fix her hurt; I could not fix mine either. Knowing that my daughter would be deeply hurt if I died, I tried hard to get my emotions under control to maintain my health. I wanted to project an "everything is going to be fine" attitude for her sake. I wanted to be healthy and happy, I wanted to laugh, but I did not know how to fix myself.

My religious beliefs made me feel like a failure. I thought that the ideal response to all circumstances was to rejoice and trust in God's sovereign plan. The pain in my heart and chest would cause me to double over and kneel, hunched over my knees. I would cry out to God to take away the pain. I had no idea how to deal with the grief.

I found that distraction and busyness could fill my mind and give me some relief, so I began to fill my life with activities to distract myself. I filled my days with never-ending to-do lists. I tried to heal my emotions and return to feeling normal, which to me meant feeling the same way I did when Tom was alive. My outward presentation was a facade. I would smile and try to create a happy home for Britney. I took her to the fair and then to Disneyland, and we would spend the entire day riding every ride. I did not want her to suffer any more loss; I wanted to be present for her. But inside I was not alive; there was no joy. My heart had closed the day Tom died. It went to the place I envisioned as heaven. I knew that I needed to change but was at a loss as to how to accomplish that.

When we had been without Tom for two years, Britney was still struggling with loss and grief, as was I. I searched for help and found a bereavement support group at our local hospital. We attended night meetings for a year; I was in the adult group, and she was in the children's group. I noticed that my daughter found comfort in the company of another little girl like her who had lost her dad in almost the same way she had.

One evening the group leader for the adults brought a bowl of rocks with comforting words engraved on them. We were each to take one rock from the bowl. I chose TRUST. It was a nice gesture on the part of the group leader, so I felt a bit ashamed that I did not appreciate the rock. As I walked away from the meeting with that rock, my thoughts trickled out. A rock! Is this all I have left of Tom?

SEARCH FOR PEACE

I subscribed to an online newsletter written by a Christian chiropractor. He always had encouraging things to say, exercises to help mobility, helpful recipes, and personal stories to share. One week in his newsletter, he shared some books that had greatly helped him during his life. One of those books was *You Can Heal Your Life* by Louise L. Hay. I went to the Goodwill store, and there was her book, waiting for me.

As I read her words, I discovered they were lifting my spirits. It was one of the first books I had read that was not based directly on the Bible. Her words reflected many of the same concepts that were in scripture. That made me comfortable, because old fears were still intact and I did not want to be led astray. In the churches I had attended, I had heard many warnings about sticking with the Bible and staying away from "false doctrine." Reading Louise Hay's suggestions, I made mental notes and compared what she said to the Bible.

The book said things that were similar to the Bible, only in different words. This new wording was lifting me; it was inspiring me and giving me hope. Hay shared simple phrases to speak out loud to nurture yourself. One phrase was "I approve of myself." When I repeated the suggested affirmations out loud, they soothed my spirit and encouraged me.

The Bible says, "Love others as you love yourself." I had focused on loving others but had never really focused on loving myself. I had never learned how to do that. Her book was like a blueprint for how to nurture and love oneself. The affirmations were giving me strength and helping me feel alive again. I was learning from her how to meet my own need.

At the same time that I discovered Louise L. Hay and her books, I was trying to find where I fit in my church family. Our church had Sunday services and also midweek gatherings where people would meet up in private homes. These midweek meetings strengthened relationships within the church. Laymen who were called house church leaders would oversee the midweek meetings. Tom and I had led a house church while he was alive. I had turned our house church over to our assistants after Tom passed on.

I needed to find a house church where my daughter and I could attend. Each house church catered to a specific group of people. There were groups for high school age, college age, young marrieds, and so on. Church members could choose to go to any house group that was open to them and met their needs. The people had potluck meals, discussed Bible themes, and shared life events. My situation was unique because I was a fifty-nine-year-old widow with a nine-year-old daughter. No group met the needs of us both. I ignored my need and selected a house church that catered to young married couples. My daughter would be able to interact with the young girls who attended there.

The leader and his wife were a young married couple. One week the house church leader approached me. He knew Tom and I had led a house church. He said, "There must be a reason that God put you in our group. Would you be the one to share something with the group next week?"

I pondered and prayed about what I should share. I had been studying self-love and self-nurture in Louise Hay's book. I knew that the wording was different from the Bible, but I saw the principle was the same. The Bible said we were to love ourselves, and Louise suggested practical ways to do that. I worked hard at preparing my talk. I used Bible scripture, and I also shared the refreshing new insights I had found in her book. I shared ways to love oneself.

The young leader said nothing to me, but I soon learned that he disapproved of what I had shared at the house church meeting. I had used a book that did not reference the Bible, and he had taken his concerns to our regional pastor, who oversaw the house church leaders in our region.

Our regional pastor was in his seventies, a wise, experienced man who knew me well. Tom and I had attended many prayer and Bible study meetings in his home. The day I picked out Tom's coffin and made burial arrangements, he had been with me. He had spent time with me trying to help me navigate my new life as a widow. He had told me his own story of loss. His wife of forty-seven years had died instantly from a brain aneurism. He had since remarried but was well aware of what it meant to be a widow and trying to heal the hurt.

The regional pastor asked if I would come and talk with him. He explained that the house leader had concerns because I was not being "biblical." He listened as I described what had transpired from my point of view. I told him that I felt angry for being judged by a young man who had no idea what I was going through. I wanted to be left in peace to grieve my loss in my way. I did not have the desire nor the energy to try to explain myself to the insensitive young leader. I asked the pastor to get him off my back. The regional pastor agreed with me and said, "You do have a right to grieve your loss in your way; it is not his business; I will handle it."

This incident was similar to the experience I had had when I was sixteen. I remembered how happy I was then when I read that Edgar Cayce could receive holistic remedies that enabled people to heal. Once again, a book other than the Bible had given me some joy. I quit attending that young man's house church. I did not want his restricting judgment to destroy the tiny shred of joy I had found. I continued to help myself by practicing the affirmations in *You Can Heal Your Life*. I had changed and no longer needed the approval of others to know what was good for me. That house church incident was the beginning of my feeling that I did not belong in the church.

※

After Tom's passing, donations from family and church families paid the portion of the funeral expenses I could not cover. Tom was a veteran, and the VA covered some of the cost. Advisors guided me, and soon I was receiving surviving spouse Social Security benefits. A friend at church approached me about an opportunity for me to earn more income. The job involved child care in the homes of two female optometrists. Their homes were not far from mine; the pay was generous, $100 per hour. Each mother had an infant and a toddler. The mothers were grateful to have a mature, experienced woman watching over their darling children.

I took care of the children during the day and was home before my daughter returned from school. Walks in the sunshine, pushing the stroller through the park, and playing with the children were ideal for me. The children's sweet spirits were a balm to my heart, and it comforted me to look after them. Tom's life on earth was over, but the lives of these four little children had just begun. I was so grateful that God had provided the extra income in such a stress-free manner.

I cared for the children for about a year after Tom died. Then the day came when my life events and child care were not syncing anymore. I knew it was time to transition. I was looking into my future, knowing my daughter would come of age and leave home. I would be alone, and I was not good at being alone. I planned to upgrade my skills and get a job in graphic design so I could be around people. I discontinued child care and started attending displaced homemaker class at Clark College while Britney was at school, then started taking part-time classes at Washington State University to upgrade my skills in digital technology and graphic design. When my daughter left home, I would be ready. I planned to distract myself from an empty home by returning to the working world.

A little more than three years after Tom passed, I became aware that the government was closing the window on short sales for homes, which Tom had thought might be the way to go in our situation. My mortgage, like all the others caught in the housing windfall, was upside down. I had no desire to move. Everywhere I looked in the house, it brought up memories of us working side by side. I loved flowers and gardens and had filled my backyard with many varieties of plants. I cherished the memories and the sweet haven we had created together.

On my own after twenty years of Tom's handling all the details of our housing, I remembered Tom's thoughts on short selling and decided to take action even though I had no experience in selling or buying a home. I found that with my Social Security income, I was eligible for a home loan. My banker assured me I could find a three-bedroom home that fit my financial picture. I found a realtor who specialized in short sales. She had a partner who searched the market to find a home I could afford. My home was a clean little jewel, and a buyer soon made an offer.

There was one hitch: I had a septic system, and the buyer, who was a single mom, was concerned about it. She wanted me to pay to have it inspected. My realtor objected and said, "In short sales, you are gaining nothing, so you do not have to pay for anything!" I asked Spirit for guidance and heard,

Pay for the septic inspection. The inspection cost me $90 and the septic was in perfect condition. The house sold on October 11, 2011. I was given thirty days to vacate.

I had bid on a foreclosed home, but my bid was still in limbo. It did not seem reasonable to me that Spirit would have me rent an apartment while waiting for my bid to be accepted. That would involve a lot of hassle, finding an apartment, storing furniture, and then moving everything again. I expected everything to go smoothly and to get the home I had bid on. I sorely missed Tom's wisdom.

A church friend who had a six-bedroom home offered to let me and my daughter stay in her home until the bid on the foreclosure was accepted. My household things went into storage except for the basics we needed while waiting for the bid approval. We set up our queen air mattress in my friend's basement bedroom. We had some clothes and two plastic three-drawer dressers. At night, whenever my daughter got up to go to the bathroom, she would fall back into the bed on her return. The air mattress would rebound on my side, and I would bounce into the air on her impact.

Days passed, then weeks, and I began bidding on other homes. One, two, three, four homes…each time someone outbid me, even when I bid more than the asking price. I was baffled; I could not understand what Spirit was doing. Why were all my bids failing to get us a house? One night I lay awake. My daughter was moving a lot in her sleep. With her every move, the air mattress would rise and fall under me. We were both uncomfortable in this situation. I thought to myself, This is crazy. Tom would never have taken the risk that I took. He would have moved us safely into an apartment until we found the home we wanted. He would not have assumed a housing bid would close at the last minute. I began talking, "Lord, we would not be in this situation if Tom had been here." I heard the response quite clearly: *I would have told you if you had asked.*

Then I realized how far off base I had gotten. It was true; I had never asked for guidance. I had assumed, and I had made a wrong decision. I now knew I needed to get my daughter into a stable situation until I secured a home. We had been in limbo for six months, sleeping on an air mattress, our possessions in storage. As I walked the hall upstairs, I overheard my host asking their lender to be patient. They had come into financial difficulty. I had been in their home six months and had very few expenses. I quickly wrote out a check for the amount he needed and handed it to him. I was glad that I had money to help them at a time of their need. It was a minor consolation that my being in their home at that time had benefited them in some way. Spirit is so very clever. I had just learned a valuable lesson, and my hosts had their need supplied. It was a tidy setup by the universe.

I took immediate action and located a suitable apartment for my daughter and me. After we moved in, I said to her, "I don't know why we did not get any of the four houses I bid on, but I do know this; we will understand in time. There is always a good reason why things happen the way they do." I did not forget the lesson. In the days ahead, when I faced a decision, I asked for wisdom and guidance. I was wiser and better suited to be the head of the household now.

PERFECT TIMING

I was a widow, a student, and a single mom. I was also trying to be a good daughter to my elderly mother. She was a veteran's widow, so I went to the Veterans Administration to see if she qualified for any benefits. I spoke to the man in charge of the VA office. We talked about my mom's situation for a while, and then he began talking about his service days in Vietnam. I mentioned that my late husband was also a veteran who had served in Vietnam. He pursued the topic and asked how Tom died. When I told him, the veteran pulled out a list of the diseases affecting and killing Vietnam veterans exposed to Agent Orange during their service. He handed me papers and asked me to fill them out.

Six weeks later, I received a large envelope in the mail from the VA. I read the letter with astonishment. The VA had determined that Tom's death was service related and awarded me a retroactive veteran's pension! The award was for three years back pay, with veterans' benefits that included a VA home loan.

The benefits also covered the cost of college classes for me and for Britney when she left high school. I returned to the gentleman who had asked me to fill out the paperwork and showed him the letter. He was delighted for me and said, "Now you can get any house you want!"

I went to my bank loan processor and showed him my change in income due to the pension. He calculated my new loan amount. I searched in the school district my daughter desired and found a home I could afford, in perfect condition. The home inspector told me he had never inspected a home like this where he could find nothing wrong. It was the estate of a physician, and his children were selling it. I bid on it, and my banker forwarded the request for loan approval to his superiors. Soon he called, and the gravity in his voice told me something was wrong. "The bank will not approve the loan."

I was stunned. "Why not?"

His response was sad and kind. "Many people have been deceitfully short selling their homes to take advantage of the fall in the housing market. They sell, get out of their upside-down mortgage, and then move into a better home that has fallen in price. The bank assumes you are manipulating the system. I know you are not, but they won't budge." This response came from the bank where I had done business for seventeen years.

I had to withdraw my offer on the house. Shortly after this disappointing news, Reno, one of my church's elders and lay pastors, called me to see how I was doing. He was one of those who had come over to my home shortly after Tom passed. I told him about the loan rejection when I bid on the house. He responded, "Maybe I can be of help." Reno was also a mortgage broker. He encouraged me by telling me a dream he had had. "In my dream, there was a wall in front of me; when I placed my hand on the wall, it began to melt away." Reno said, "God has been giving me favor helping people get into homes." He took on the challenge and asked me for the address of the home I wanted.

As it turned out, the home was still on the market. To my way of thinking, that was a bit of a miracle in itself. The price was below market, and the home was perfect. Reno began his work and plowed through every difficulty he encountered. He could personally vouch for my integrity because he had known my husband and me for several years. I was praying up a storm that

God would give me the house, and this time, I could feel the wind of Spirit behind my prayers. I shouted out loud as I drove down the freeway, "God, please give me that house."

Miraculously, Reno obtained the loan for me and then guided me in how to bid. The realtor selling the home was indignant that I would bid on the house again. She felt burned because my bank had refused the loan on my first bid, so she refused to accept this second bid. Reno unblinkingly forged forward, saying, "She is going to buy a house; it will be the one you are selling or another one, but she will buy a house." That did it. The realtor caved in, and I got the house! My realtor had been with me through the four failed bids and was as ecstatic as I. She told me that she had shared my story with other realtors and they were telling my story to encourage their clients.

The best part about this story is that I did not want any of the four previously bid-on homes. I was settling for the best I could find within my Social Security income. They were what I could afford. When my income increased through the VA pension and loan benefits, I found a home I wanted and loved. The house was perfect for me, and I was buying it under market price. I remembered what I had told my daughter. "There is a good reason my bids on four homes did not get accepted." Now we knew the reason; God had a home for us that we both would love. We just had to wait for the right time when all the events came together.

※

Britney and I enjoyed our beautiful new home. We benefited from the VA pension and retroactive pay in multiple ways. Using the VA discount, we went to Maui one year and Disneyland the next. Britney wanted to play violin, and I could afford to buy her a violin and pay for private lessons. She excelled in music and had artistic talent. The VA benefits also allowed me to attend WSU for three years and take all the core courses required for a bachelor's degree in digital technology. I was on track with my survival plan.

Even though I was enjoying all the blessings that come with financial freedom, the loss of Tom was still painful. When all the busy activity of life's music shut off, I felt the empty hole inside. Somehow I believed the emptiness was my fault. I reasoned that if my relationship with God and the universe were strong enough, I would not feel alone. I did not know how to fix myself and asked God to help me find the remedy.

Since his death in July 2009, I had tried each year to create scrapbook albums of Tom's life. I wanted to make three quality albums, one for each stepson and one for my daughter. There were six grandchildren, and I did not want Tom to become an unknown grandfather with no trace of his history. From 2009 to 2013, my attempts to organize, duplicate the photos, and create the albums had failed. Every time I attempted the project, the grief would surface and drain every ounce of strength from my being. I would close the box full of photos, memory cards, and condolence cards and put it away.

Before Tom's memorial service in 2009, I was asked if I had a request to add to the program. I requested that people write down the memorable times they had had with Tom. A dear woman volunteered to create custom-decorated blank cards and hand them out to the memorial service attendees. Tom had had a wonderful gift of lifting people's spirits with his positive perspective on life. He would say things that transformed mindsets for the better. How well I knew, he often did that for me. At the service, people took the decorated blank cards and wrote their stories about how he had helped and encouraged them. All the memorial cards were in my Tom box. I had read the happy stories many times.

In 2014 while at WSU taking digital technology classes, I learned how to create and edit videos. New inspiration sparked within me as I discovered that making videos came naturally to me. I immediately recognized this new tool as an additional method to help compile Tom's life history for the children. With my newfound technology and inspiration, I opened the Tom box once again. This time, the memory cards and letters about him warmed my heart instead of breaking it open. The process of creating the video and making the albums shifted my perspective so that I now thanked God for the twenty years I had enjoyed with this good man. I focused on the blessing rather than on his death and the loss. This time as I worked on making the albums, the inspiration flowed out. The energy was with me; I was once again back on track.

When Christmas 2014 arrived, I had completed the albums and the video; five years had passed since his death in 2009. Britney was bravely finding her way forward in life, excelling on her violin, making friends, and deciding which college courses she would take after high school graduation. The personalized album I made for Britney contained photos of sweet, tender moments between her and her daddy. She appreciated having the album to freshen her memories of the fun times she had had with him.

I opened my Facebook page and posted the freshly completed video honoring Tom. The response was gratifying. More than five hundred people viewed and enjoyed that video. His warm, outgoing nature, friendly smile, and amusing jokes had been enjoyed by many, and he was being remembered for them. I was happy to have finally been able to complete my desire to honor his life. I was no longer grieving about Tom but instead was enjoying the memories of him.

8

Ready to Love Again

I was sixty-five and no longer the naive youth dependent on others to guide my life. Life had given me gifts: Tom, my daughter, miraculous healings, and many answered prayers. I still had unresolved emotions from losing loved ones; I hated death and separation. The emptiness I felt inside was a mystery to me. Was I making some error and in some way responsible? If so, I had no clue how to correct it. Jesus had taught, "I have come that they might have life and that they might have it more abundantly." Love and respect for Spirit, that I knew, but abundant life seemed to have eluded my grasp.

The switch from grief to gratefulness came after I found closure with Tom. Peace started to trickle in, and hope sprang up as my heart opened. I began to believe I could love again. Am I a person who is better off with a companion? Is that why I feel empty when alone? I was opening to the future and letting go of the past. I felt positive, expectant energy when I prayed for guidance to find a new companion.

On January 1, 2015, I placed my profile on the Match.com dating site. Immediately I began getting invitations. I looked at faces and read profiles. Nothing clicked; I just felt no, no, no, no. I wanted a widower who could relate to having loved and lost. Then I saw a photo of Mark garbed head to toe in fishing gear, walking in a river. He seemed to be an earth man, a person like me who loved nature. His writing revealed an intelligent, thoughtful, spiritual person with a sense of humor. On January 4, I sent him an email greeting.

Mark responded almost immediately. "This evening, I consumed your profile; I always enjoy photos, and yours display a healthy, happy, lovely lady with a beautiful smile, and the text of your profile is indeed aligned with my desires. So, what might be our next step, Diana? I enjoy a little email dialogue, then a meeting for coffee, and a chemistry test. :-) I tend to be a little bit slow and deliberate (patient) as we move through getting to know you, and I ask that we allow our God to set the pace and direct the process. Easy. :-) Oh, I do like to do a telephone interface when the spirit moves us. So, I'll look forward to sharing emails, as often as daily if you like."

I enjoyed his use of words. His smiley faces created with keyboard strokes added warmth to his text. We continued happy emails for three more days, sharing lighthearted tidbits.

DIVINE GUIDANCE

On January 7, the tone changed; Mark sent me a lengthy email that revealed he struggled with underlying concerns. He was wavering about the unknowns and possible difficulties of developing a new relationship. He knew he was in some form of life transition and was very desirous that time and circumstance take control.

I read and reread his email and the journal notes he shared, mulling his baffling fluctuations back and forth. What was he saying? Did he want to stop emailing? I used a highlighter to mark the portions of the email where he was clearly hoping to find love and companionship. "Diana, I have no idea what tomorrow may bring, and I love the mystery of that. So, if you are moved to send me a note, if we find our lives drawn mysteriously closer, I am excitedly waiting upon and anticipating whatever might occur."

The emotion of his text felt to me like a drowning person hoping someone would see his hand breaking the surface of the water, perhaps for the last time. He did not reveal the cause of his heavy heart, but I knew he was in trouble. Not sure how to proceed, I prayed for guidance and received a mental image while in prayer. I had not yet met Mark face to face. In the vision, I saw a man I knew represented Mark. He wore blue jeans and a work shirt. He was kneeling on the ground, sitting back on his calves. He appeared to be praying, his head down, his shoulders drooping slightly forward. His hands were clasped together and resting on top of his thighs. I could feel the heaviness of his burden as I approached him from the back. Standing slightly behind him on his left, I extended my right hand toward him. Mine was a gesture of help, friendship, and encouragement.

The vision ended, and I knew what I should do. Mark needed hope and a friend to help him through a time of weariness. I searched the internet and found a sad trail of events in his history. His deceased wife had spiraled downward due to drugs, physical illness, and body wounds that would not heal; she was facing a possible court indictment for a drug-related felony. She left home and disappeared, and later her body was found in the river. I felt led to continue with Mark and gently remove his concerns about developing a relationship. The soul of this man captured my attention. I liked his manner of communication, honesty, and desire for simplicity and peace.

I responded to Mark, "My brother, my friend, God has given you a beautiful heart. I feel as though you have placed a piece of your precious soul in my hand. I do not want to damage or harm it in any way. I carefully read what you shared from your journaling; we agree on letting God be God and letting him work his wonders. I offer this suggestion if you feel inclined. Contact me and let me come your way to see your piece of paradise and river house. I would love to meet you, sit by the stream, and talk. We live about an hour apart; with GPS, I won't get lost. Mark, thank you for your transparency. I am a good listener when you need one."

Mark wrote back quickly, happy that I was willing to visit on his turf. He felt a need to prepare me for what I might expect. In 2000, he and his wife had purchased the home on the river when his architectural business was thriving, with grand plans to renovate. But she had struggled with and succumbed to old addictions and unresolved childhood pain, leading in 2007 to what was suspected to be a suicide drowning. Eight years had since passed, but Mark was only just beginning to find peace and move forward again. He was a man of order and perfection, and now felt embarrassed about his unrenovated home.

He wrote, "Diana, I greatly enjoy your notes, and there is some genuine pull towards you. Your notes exude a soft loving quality, which I am very much drawn to, and last night, the moon was on the river, reflecting from a muted midnight blue sky. Silver-white sparkles fell on the river, and the whole canyon was alive with a natural light show. It is tremendously exhilarating when creation dances before you with amazing natural splendor. I wish it were something I could share; photography leaves it void of soul; it is a place in paradise. I am delighted that you might consider visiting my river home."

He explained that he had spent the last three years and all his savings renovating the family home he had inherited in 2011, which he called the Farmhouse. He was seventeen years old when his father started building the Farmhouse, and working on that project had launched Mark into building and architecture. Renovating the Farmhouse now was a tribute to his father. He sent photos of the renovation, and I could see that Mark's considerable skills were transforming the old house into a grand dwelling. But, he confided, his business had declined when the housing market fell, and now his finances were short. I suspected financial burdens made him reluctant to begin a new relationship.

"Mark, I understand how wonderful working alongside your father was," I wrote him. "My father loved carpentry, and some of that drifted over into my veins. You have such a noble heart, such desire to do the right thing; I admire your values, Mark. Those years rebuilding your parents' home are also an investment in your own heart. Money can't fill the painful voids in life. You invested your money because your heart needed to. I do not believe you will ever regret that, though it left you in a financial bind at the moment. You did a great job restoring it. You are awesome!!"

When he told me that he had listed his river house for sale, I experienced a wave of sadness that he felt a need to sell his piece of paradise. "Where would you go, where would you live if you sold it?" I asked. "An even deeper question is how could you satisfy the longing of your heart to touch and see nature if you leave this place? I can only imagine that you are doing this out of necessity rather than the desire to leave."

Mark replied, "Well, I am not certain that I will leave. One offer I accepted in October evaporated. So, I asked Christ if he wanted me elsewhere, and I opened myself to the opportunity. I have been encouraged by his response, *It is the desires of* your *heart, Mark, which we are addressing. What do you desire?* I am satisfied that I will be staying here; I will likely be rebuilding this home just as I desired when he moved us here fifteen years ago. Nonetheless, I make it a habit to remain ready for whatever I am called to do."

❃

The loneliness of widowhood is a well-known reality; to find a compatible friend and share daily life is pure gold. Mark was a rare find. The more he revealed of himself, the more I was drawn to him. Like me, he heard and trusted the Christ within. He loved nature as I did. We emailed daily, attaching photos of things we loved most. We were like two delighted children, laughing and sharing the toys we each had in our toy box.

Our comfort level grew, and we decided it was time to meet face to face. "Your writing exudes a deep genuineness of spirit, Diana. I feel as though there is indeed something of significance to this connection. So thank you for your willingness to explore further. I would consider trying to schedule a time when we might meet if that is something which would work with your busy life. :-)" I responded that it would give me great pleasure to have our first meeting at the place pictured in his photographs online, his piece of paradise on the river.

He suggested a phone call, and conversation flowed as we relished the sound of each other's voice. After the call, Mark's email revealed his enthusiasm and humor. "I think we should talk on the phone between now and our meetup day. Would that be fun? Whatdoyouthink? :-) Until we meet again, see you soon!"

I loved the homemade tilted smiley faces he inserted in the text. I emailed back, "Wednesday meet up with you, YES, YES, YES, and a phone call before that :-) YES, YES, YES." The happy emails flew back and forth, punctuated with phone calls. Two widowed people had found laughter, companionship, and common ground; we were anxious to see each other. On Wednesday,

January 14, I drove out to meet this unique man at the River House. Just as Mark had told me, the house needed repair. I had seen his website and the many beautiful homes he had designed and built. This home was not the handiwork he would have liked me to see.

I walked through the wooden gate and down the sidewalk toward the home, its unique architecture reminiscent of Snow White's cottage in the woods. Two doors; which one is correct? I knocked on the closest one, and Mark quickly came out the other door. He was all smiles, walking down the sidewalk to greet me. He spoke with evident surprise and pleasure, "You are gorgeous!" I was glad that he thought so; I felt welcomed and happy that my exterior was to his liking. I was checking him out also; he was physically fit and handsome. Now in our sixties, we both knew the brevity of life and the importance of keeping our bodies healthy and fit. We had both passed the first impressions test.

We talked for nearly four hours. January is a cold month in Oregon, and his home was chilly. Mark sat on the brick hearth, stoking his woodstove with logs. He poured out his life story, not knowing I was startled by his candid disclosures. I mentally catalogued his life events; we had arrived at this point in life having traveled very different pathways. He gave me a tour of his home and showed me his architectural models on the upper level in his workspace. From the loft we gazed through windows and watched the Molalla River flowing west toward the ocean.

We drove up the Molalla River corridor, stopping at his favorite spots. As we walked along the edge of the road, he knelt to pick out rusty nails embedded in the gravel. Only an observant eye would have seen them. I chuckled, "I do that too; I can't pass a weed in the sidewalk without stopping to pull it." We both needed everything to be in its proper place. He showed me where he had placed a garbage can, hoping people would throw their trash into it, and told me he had given up the attempt after vandals smashed the can.

Back at his house for lunch, he had prepared a wonderful salad with sautéed steelhead on the side. Conversation flowed effortlessly, enhanced by the bond that widows and widowers understand. I met his three aging pets—two cats, Blondie and Josie, and Mary, a poodle. We mildly touched on religion.

He had begun in traditional Christian churches and found the doctrines intolerable over time. "How could anyone believe that a God of love would send his children to hell?" He asked me what I knew about New Age beliefs, and I said, "Nothing," and asked him to share. Mark believed we are on earth to serve Christ by serving others. I admired his values, and he felt my acceptance of his person.

It was time for me to go, so I rose to leave. He circled momentarily in one spot and motioned for me to wait, saying, "There is something I want to show you." He left the living room, his footsteps echoing as he climbed and descended the stairs; he returned to my side with a paper in his hands. "I wrote this poem; I think you will relate to it."

Not Knowing

I rather like the joy of not knowing,
The trials of trusting, while dreaming and growing.
If life were indeed of mere human design,
Then where would be evidenced the hand of the divine?

When I said I loved the poem, he gave me the paper. Then we held hands and faced each other. I prayed briefly that God would guide us, we hugged, and he helped me into my coat. I heard the river sounds as he walked me to my car. He blew a respectful kiss as I waved goodbye. We were both cautious and looking for clues as to why Providence had brought us together. From Mark's perspective, I was the church lady. For me, I knew my religious community would not see in him what I saw. Our minds were full of questions, and our hearts were calling to each other. Back home, closing our day with a phone call, Mark revealed his heart first: "I can't quit thinking about you." "You are like a magnet to me," I told him.

The more we saw each other, the more we wanted to be together. Mark emailed his feelings. "Good evening, Diana: So, if I were to have my way with the world at this moment, I would drive over and spend the evening with you. I could stop at the store and pick up that special item for supper, and grab a movie at Red Box. Ideally, you might live in a cottage just walking distance downriver so that I could stop in on your back deck after fly fishing, and we could share the day and a glass of whatever, don't you think? Yeah, the essence of this note is simply, Gee, I wish we were closer."

"I wish you were here too. The time spent with you is delicious," I replied. His poem inspired me to write one in response.

Reflections on Not Knowing

Not knowing is a kindness
that causes us to enjoy the moment.
The warmth of another's smile,
the heartfelt tears as they share their tale.

Not knowing is a gift
that removes the weight of things unseen.
The future is best left to God, for we would err
in our efforts to alter what he decrees.

Not knowing is a delight
that thrills the heart with surprise.
To see around the bend, to peek before we should,
is to spoil the fun that God has planned.

Not knowing is safety,
waiting until Spirit shows a pathway that is firm.

Not knowing is a place of rest
within the hearts that know their God.

Not knowing,
I pause for awhile to learn God's intent.
I will rest by the stream, close my eyes,
listen to the violin, until He bids me come.

Mark came across this phrase and sent it to me: "Friends are like angels who lift us to our feet when our wings have trouble remembering how to fly." That phrase deeply moved me. We had lifted each other, and together we were remembering how to fly. I was trying to keep my heart reined in. On

January 19, 2015, I journaled, "Jesus, thank you for working with me, settling me. Thank you for my brother, Mark, who walks carefully before you." Voice within: *He is more than a brother.* As I heard those words, I also understood the tone of voice. It meant, I know that you are aware of what you find in your heart; he is more to you than a brother.

I would have to face and ignore five decades of religious conditioning if I chose Mark. Mark was free from people's opinions; such opinions had bound me for a lifetime. I knew that meeting Mark was the hand of my God, challenging me to follow my heart and quit letting others control my choices. Then I had a dream. I was standing and speaking to Mark. I said to him, "I have reached a point in life where I am ready to laugh, to love, and to live again."

※

February came, and I began taking lunch to Mark and helping him with the Farmhouse renovation. We delighted in working together, smiling at each other through glass panes, each polishing our side of the window. He meticulously checked his newly installed doors, calling to me, "Come see this." He kneeled and gently pushed the door; it effortlessly glided forward and clicked shut. He smiled with pleasure at his handiwork. "Notice: the door closes softly; every section is aligned perfectly, no hindrances anywhere." I admired his attention to detail, architectural knowledge, and integrity; he did his work with precision and love.

We sat down for lunch, and I noticed large tears seep out and trickle down his cheeks. They came without provocation; he made no mention of them. I knew full well the pain that pushed out that kind of tears; they were tears of loss. I had shed those tears for my father, baby Brock, and Tom. Those tears come when you give away your heart and it gets broken. Mark struggled to let go of his past as we forged our relationship. We knew our differences but trusted the synchronicities that had brought us together. We observed each other with curiosity as our perceptions enlarged.

Mark began to experience an opening of his heart. He emailed, "I am learning, or perhaps accepting, aligning, becoming new again. You, Diana, are softly ushering into my world a new perspective. Each of us has enjoyed a life career as dedicated servants of this corporate Kingdom, each with our own area and perspectives. Now, we find ourselves reassigned, together, to a new venture, one which seems oddly different to each of us and as yet uncertain. Nonetheless, we have placed our faith in the corporate Kingdom, loyal servants for a lifetime. We trust even this seemingly odd reassignment, and I am happy to be here with you."

I emailed back, "Meeting and helping you is one of the most blessed assignments I have been privileged to walk in. The oil of joy has been my portion since we met."

Mark and I had a powerful bond, a foundation stone, that caused us to rejoice that we had found each other. It was our mutual love relationship with Jesus. We freely shared our spiritual experiences. When he told me one time, "Diana, there is no hell," I was happy to hear his views about reincarnation. Perhaps there was no angry God after all. I said, "I hope you're right, Mark. I have never understood the contradiction between a God of love and hell. If reincarnation is true, there is no need for hell."

Watching his relationship with Christ caused me to imagine people worldwide, each serving Spirit their own way. My views were changing. Mark commented, "We are not so different, you and I."

❈

On the first day I met Mark in person, he had startled me by sharing his sexual encounters, from his teenage years up through the time of his marriage. Though surprised, I left his home that day knowing I could trust him. He was not a liar; having no fear of people's opinions, he had no motive to lie. In our first two months, we bantered in a gentle battle regarding this topic of sex.

Mark had an Adam-and-Eve mindset of monogamy; two people in love were to flow with the emotions they felt for each other. Love was to be natural, organic, fun and spontaneous, devoid of civilization's ceremonies and constraints. He desired sexual intimacy to evolve as naturally as the river flowed downstream. He would slip hints into our emails, playfully suggesting our meetings be followed by wild sex. His words shocked me, so I ignored him at first. He persisted, and I responded in exasperated rebuttal, "Mark, will you stop the wild sex talk. You know how I feel about this." "I am just trying to keep the conversation fun," he responded.

My conditioning put a high value on abstinence before marriage. I had come to believe refraining from premarital sex was a gift of virtue a woman gave to the man she loved. I struggled to realize I had met a man who did not see any value in my being chaste. In my religious community, I had reached the pinnacle of perfection, but in Mark's worldview, I was out of sync with the natural order of life.

One day we were at his house, and he had prepared a nice soup-and-salad lunch. After eating, we sat on the couch to talk. He smiled, "Want to get naked?" Shocked, amused, slightly indignant, I looked him square in the eye, not believing he had the nerve to be so out-of-the-blue blatant. He was dead serious! "No-o-o." I meant it; I had never been with anyone who talked like he did. I mentally made excuses for his behavior. Is he just being an adult? Is this a valid question? I never knew when he was going to pop the questions or hints.

"Are you orgasmic?"

"Yes, of course, but I can't believe that you just asked me that!"

Another day, I was leaving after a visit, and Mark chose a path that led by his washing machine. He raised the lid of the washer and said, "I put clean sheets on the bed." I said nothing and continued toward my car; Mark walked at my side. When I was in my car, ready to leave, he leaned into my open car window and said, "You sure are a strong woman."

On another visit, Mark and I sat on the couch talking. I thought I would make my position very clear. "Mark, I don't do sex before marriage." He shot straight up off the couch like a rocket and exclaimed, "I don't do marriage before sex!" He marched off toward the kitchen, his arms moving in rhythm like a wound-up toy. He turned the corner, out of my sight, marched through the laundry room, and reappeared seconds later, having gone full circle.

I sat on the couch, wondering what was coming next. He plunked down again beside me and smiled sweetly, "Now I don't want you to go home and never come back." We were both equally amused and bemused by our co-created drama. Our impasse caused mental turmoil within both of us. The higher intelligence that had brought us together was stretching us both to the limit. Mark had tried his best tactics and logic to lure me into his arms. He paced the floor, turning circles, "You and your damn rules. It is through sex that we grow love."

"I disagree; love comes first. Sex is not a method of exploration or play to find out if we love each other. Sex follows commitment; I can't give the deepest part of myself to someone until I know they are deeply in love with and committed to me." I was not going to let Mark, religion, or my family decide this matter for me. I went to prayer, found my answer of peace, returned to Mark, and explained what I needed to enter a lifetime relationship.

We worked through our different viewpoints. He said to me, "You are making a better man out of me." Another time he said, "I am proud to be seen with you."

In the end, we both got what we wanted.

※

Glorious sunshine flooded Mark's lower yard on March 8, 2015. We followed the path leading to the river and stood beside a giant fir tree. The river sounds and warm sunshine greeted us; we stood hand in hand facing the blue sky. We shared our vows of love and asked God to guide us until death parted us. In June 2015, we announced our engagement and set a date for our marriage, March 12, 2016. Mark and I spent the great majority of 2015 completing the renovation of the Farmhouse. We planned to sell it and use the funds to renovate the River House.

We wrote our own vows and bought matching rings. On March 11, 2016, the day before our wedding, Mark and I went up to the Farmhouse to arrange the living room for our short ceremony. We clowned, danced, and kissed before my video camera in a mock dress rehearsal. On March 12, we were married in the Farmhouse we had renovated together. Four family members assisted. Britney played her violin, and my mother was my bridesmaid. Mark's brother was his best man, and his sister-in-law filmed the ceremony. Reno, my friend, lay pastor, realtor, and loan officer of my home, performed the ceremony.

The song "A Thousand Years" by Christina Perri played while we stood facing each other in front of our loved ones, Reno, and God. "I have loved you for a thousand years. I'll love you for a thousand more." Mark wore blue jeans and a casual tan jacket with a white carnation in the buttonhole; I wore a softly draping longish white sweater and a knee-length navy blue skirt and held a bouquet of white carnations, soft pink Peruvian lilies, and fern fronds. "I rejoice today because God chose you for me…. My life is complete when you are with me," I pronounced in my vow. "The love of Christ, which creates and sustains all things, provides for those of us who desire it a place of perfect love here and now, and our loving arms are that place, truly and eternally," said Mark in his.

Later in June, we invited all our family and friends to the Farmhouse for our reception. We looked forward to spending our golden years together.

9

Newlywed to Newly Widowed

Mark was an award-winning Molalla River steward helping three nonprofit organizations—Molalla River Watch, Molalla River Alliance, and Native Fish Society—preserve the rivers and native fish. As guru over his domain, he knew the location of every redd (spawning place in the gravel on the river bottom) where the steelhead salmon laid their eggs. I loved walking the river with him, counting redds and embracing the quiet music of the forest. One day as we followed animal trails through the woods toward the river, Mark suddenly sprinted forward and hid behind a tree. Delighted, I followed his cue and ran to find my hiding place. We darted through the forest like children, finding and losing each other again and again. He loved to make memories, transforming the mundane into the magical. It was that passion and excitement for life that had drawn me to him.

Mark was as genuine, wild, and changing as the river. When angered, he spoke his mind freely, like water crashing into rocks in the torrent. After he had said his piece, he moved on like a gentle stream. Authenticity, bravery, and service to others were attributes he modeled. Government corruption and greed distressed him; mother nature and the natural order were his utopias.

By contrast, I was like a deep pool that revealed my depth to no one. My chosen path was peace making, fairness, and service to others. For many years I had memorized proverbs, and when I was faced with conflict, the scriptures guided my response. I lived by words like "A soft answer turns away wrath," "Anger rests in the bosom of fools," "To start a quarrel is to release a flood, so abandon the dispute before it breaks out." I refrained from speaking unless I could say something wise or beneficial to all involved. I saw critical tongues and explosive anger as traps that destroyed relationships. I let down my guard only with animals and nature because they had no guile or malice.

Every relationship has something to teach us, and we learn from each other. Mark did not understand my unruffled silence, and one night at dinner, he and Britney chimed in together, "Why do you get so quiet?" They were comrades in freely expressing their opinions. I had not found the freedom they knew, and they waited for my answer. "I don't like to react if something upsets me. I like to think before I respond. I don't want to say anything that will be hurtful to another."

※

After our wedding, Mark continued to be Mark, freely expressing his frustration. His fiery darts of anger sometimes came in my direction. My shield of protection was growing thinner, and his words stung. One night I was unable to sleep, and tears seeped from my eyes as he lay next to me peacefully slumbering. I remembered the five years of loneliness after Tom died. I thought, These painful emotions are worse than feeling alone. Recalling Tom's big bear hugs, his easy-to-be-with nature, I said to myself, Tom, I need a hug.

In the world I knew, husbands did not talk to their wives as Mark did to me. I never intentionally provoked him and knew I did not deserve unkind words. I had spent a lifetime honing my skills, trying to fit perfectly into the roles people wanted me to play. I knew I could do no better; something had to change. I left the bedroom, consoled myself in prayer, and returned to his side. To my dismay, the tears and pain came again. I got up and repeated the process, only to discover that the painful emotions surfaced again each time I returned to his side. At 2:00 a.m., I rose again to search the internet. I found that Mark's words were verbal abuse, and professionals would label me a victim. It was time for me to talk to Mark.

The next morning Mark was up and dressed early. I was in the bathroom combing my hair when Mark strode in smiling and presented me with a gift of cut fruit and steaming tea. I accepted his gift, thanked him, and began softly speaking the words I had mentally rehearsed. As I described my experience from the night before, we stood face to face, our toes nearly touching. His kind eyes looked deeply into mine as he patiently waited for me to continue. "I am a tender flower that needs gentle words that fall like rain. Our love is in its infancy, a delicate structure, like strands of a spider web. Each day the web can be made stronger by adding new strands. When you shout at me, those delicate strands of love are torn loose from their anchor. It is as though you swing your hand, break the web, and destroy the tender masterpiece in one swift motion. I have to work hard to repair the brokenness and weave new strands."

He was unaware that his angry outbursts had hurt me. He smiled, paused thoughtfully, and said, "If we were under attack, wouldn't you want a strong man who could defend you?" I remembered his story; he was bullied as a child and when his family turned a deaf ear to his cries for relief, he had chosen to fight back. He was small for his age but had a lion's heart. When the bullies attacked, he fought them off, breaking knuckle bones in both hands; he was never bothered by any bullies again. Anger was an ally he found useful. He saw himself as a warrior taking a righteous stance. Those were reasons I loved him; he was true to himself and brave.

"Of course, Mark, but I should not need to be protected from you," I replied.

"I will need to ponder on this," he answered.

I must have been the first person to challenge his behavior lovingly. He understood my perspective and knew I was not criticizing him. To his credit, he never spoke to me in anger again. He reserved his shouting for obstacles of life that frustrated him. One day when I was helping him with one of his projects, he erupted in anger and frustration. I quickly assessed the situation and opted to let him solve his problem alone. I smiled and cheerfully informed him, "I'm going downstairs now. If you need my help, just let me know." Later that day, he spoke to me with admiration: "You handled that well." He saw, through my actions, another way to deal with emotion rather than a full-throttle explosion. He let me know he approved of the way I acted under fire, telling me one time, "You are sure easy to get along with; I like it."

※

We enjoyed the gifts each had brought into the marriage. Mark was a servant and a rescuer, and his mechanical, carpentry, and design skills dazzled me. He could repair anything. One day I accidentally dropped a pearl earring and groaned in dismay as it spiraled down the bathroom sink drain. Mark was off to the rescue immediately. He crawled under the house, took the drain apart, and returned beaming with the earring in his hand. He loved to serve and was thrilled at the opportunity to rescue.

I had accounting skills, and he was relieved that I kept the books. I enjoyed yardwork and cooking; presenting three home-cooked meals each day was my joy. He expressed his gratitude at various times. "God has answered all of my prayers through you." "You take such good care of me. If I had known you could cook this well, I would have married you sooner." He reflected on the sorrowful seven years he had lived with a functioning addict. "I'm sure glad you are not an addict."

Mark had spent a lifetime being true to himself; he was authentic, a hammer of truth. I had spent a lifetime being what others wanted; I was a people pleaser, a dove of peace. Mark began tapping his hammer on my shell of reserve; his authenticity antennae sensed I had buried a part of myself. He perceived that I was performing a role I thought others wanted. Without criticism, he kindly pointed out what I failed to see: "You think you are perfect." He was right; I was doing my best to be perfect. No one had ever wanted me to be the real me.

Mark knew I was a caged bird and desired to set me free. "There is an untamed, natural femininity within you; it is within every woman." He tugged on the cage door that bound me, trying to free me from learned rules, past reprimands, accumulated fear, and joy-sapping restraint. He wanted to create a deeper heart-and-soul connection between us and beckoned me to open up, offering himself as a friend I could trust. "Don't you want to be close? Don't you want deep intimacy? Have you never had a friend that you confided in, someone you could trust and be open with?"

"No, Mark, I never have."

I was distressed; I did not know how to be what he asked me to be, how to be what I had never let myself become. I had left the authentic Diana behind long ago. She was lost, and I did not know who she was or where to find her. This man I loved did not see my best performance as perfection; he saw it as a barrier between us. My mind searched for solutions. For a lifetime, I had performed, striving to meet everyone's expectations, denying my own needs, tilting the scales in favor of others. In so doing, I had paid the price of ignoring and imprisoning my own heart. I had so silenced my inner fire that I could no longer find it or hear it. Indeed, I had forgotten it existed. Mark wanted to free my spirit but did not have the skills to break the bars that bound the caged dove, and neither did I.

And while Mark wanted me to be a free spirit emotionally, he controlled every creative effort I made. He wanted to be the leader in the aesthetics of the home. He had known free rein and earned high praise for his architectural skills. His clients with unlimited budgets were thrilled with his masterpieces. His designer eye spread beyond his workspace into the house, yard, and world, seeking perfection and alignment everywhere. His accomplishments encouraged his belief that things would be better if done his way. I, too, had a history of success and compliments regarding my abilities to organize, keep order, and make things look better. I had been free to do things my way in the creative arena. Both JoAnn Fabrics and Tom had given me joyous free rein to make my domains look pretty. I assumed Mark would enjoy my tidiness and nesting habits.

Bit by bit I learned that my marriage to Mark was not a place of home making freedom for me. I was cleaning the kitchen sink one day when Mark walked up and stood near me. I looked up into his eyes and smiled. He pleasantly asked, "Is there a reason you put that sponge there?" Baffled, I looked at the sponge on the left side of the faucet. I knew that it had initially been on the right side.

"No."

"Don't you think it makes good sense that the sponge is kept on the right?"

"I did not think too much about it." I moved the offending sponge back, shocked that he was bothered by such a minimal issue. Mark went on his way, and Britney and I were left alone in the kitchen. We grinned incredulously as our eyes met. It's a sponge!! Her eyes rolled, and she mouthed, "OCD." This was not the first time Mark had objected when I moved something.

I mentally projected to the days ahead of me, thinking of the hundreds of ways I could transgress by innocently moving something from Mark's "good sense" location. I felt a mild panic; this was as difficult as walking on eggs without breaking them. I thought, Calm yourself; you can do this and memorize where things belong. Day followed day as I chronically battled every creative spark, every longing to rearrange, make better, and beautify. I became a holding tank of restraint. Mark's need to have his say in the proper alignment of all things was suffocating to me. This dilemma felt like a vise, and I had not developed the skills to solve the problem.

I tried to help Mark understand my joy in homemaking by comparing it to his joy in designing beautiful architecture, "Mark, how would you feel if I stood over your shoulder correcting you as you designed your homes?"

"It's not the same thing." He could not understand that he was dominating the only canvas I had never had to give up to please others. I thought, Give it time, we will find a way to work together; this is our first year. He will come to trust my abilities, loosen his grip, and let me joyfully execute some of my ideas. Another woman might have asserted herself and told him, "Forget you, I will do what I want." That was not my way. I sighed and went into "be patient" mode. I was so grateful for the blessings that came from being with Mark that patience was a small price to pay.

We found striking parallels in our lives. Williams was the maiden name of both of our mothers. We were both raised on twenty-acre farms, swam in rivers, and loved nature. We had both first married in our late thirties to divorced people with two children. Neither of us had biological children, and, amazingly, both had parented a Brock and a Britney. We had earned college degrees and loved art. He chose architectural design; I chose graphic design. We joked as we discovered our similarities, "We must be cousins."

Mark related to my Britney and understood her; he helped bring her out of the pain of losing Tom as much as he brought me out of it. He thought a kitten would bring her special joy. He had a friend whose longhaired ragdoll cat had had kittens, so the three of us went to their home and Britney picked out a male kitten as her companion. She named him Harry Pawter because he had a lightning bolt marking on his forehead, and lightning was a symbol of Harry Potter.

When Mark and I rode into town in his twenty-year-old Chevrolet pickup, the bench seat allowed me to snuggle next to him, my head on his shoulder, my left hand on his thigh. A neighbor once commented to me, "I saw you two drive by. You could not have gotten a slip of paper between the two of you." As we were doing errands in his truck one day, Mark tilted his head down and smiled at me. "I never thought I would be happy again. We are lucky, you and I, to have found love a second time."

※

Four days after our first anniversary, on March 17, 2017, Mark returned home after making an architectural presentation to a group of board members. He immediately lay down on our bed and told me, "After the meeting, I walked out of the building toward the car, and a horrible pain hit me between the shoulder blades; I almost passed out." Mark had always been active, dynamic, and vibrant, an early riser who never napped during the day. It was a sign of serious trouble to see him lying on the bed. He was experiencing alarming internal symptoms.

"Do you want to go to a doctor?"

"Yes." He then added, "This could bankrupt us."

"Mark, don't worry about the money; you are worth more to me than any amount of money. Let's take care of you."

He had no family doctor, so I drove him to Providence Immediate Care. I pulled the car close to their entryway and watched his slow steps toward the doors. I parked the car, entered the building, and searched for him in the waiting lobby. A nurse led me to a room where Mark lay on a table, surrounded by staff and attached to medical devices. The staff informed us his vital signs were alarming. He was placed on a gurney, loaded into an ambulance, and rushed to Kaiser Hospital. Soon he was in a hospital room, connected to IVs on both sides of his bed. He was in great pain. The staff informed us his blood pressure was off the charts and his aorta had a fine hairline split that ran its entire length from the heart exit to the sacrum. The split had been caused by uncontrolled high blood pressure that neither of us had been aware of. I called his brother and other family members and alerted them to the alarming turn of events.

After he seemed stabilized, I left to buy some supplies. I had barely left the hospital lot when Mark called me and said they were moving him again. They had found an aneurysm forming within his aorta, blocking blood flow to his kidneys. Back at Kaiser Hospital, I arrived to see staff wheeling him on a gurney toward a waiting ambulance. The ambulance sped him from Kaiser to Oregon Health and Science University (OHSU), where the most complex health needs in the region are treated. I followed the ambulance, hindered by dense traffic. My cell phone rang, and when I saw that the call was from OHSU, I pulled over and answered it. A doctor explained, "The blood is not getting to Mark's kidneys; he will be on dialysis for life if we do not operate immediately. We need your permission."

"Of course, do what you need to do!"

Mark was in the pre-surgery room when I arrived at the hospital; I could not see him. Mark's stepson joined me in the waiting room. Hours passed, and finally the surgeon came and led us to a private room. His face revealed concern. "The surgery went well, blood is getting to his kidneys, but there is a complication. When he woke from the anesthesia, he appeared to have what looked like a seizure. No one knows for sure what lies ahead; he is not waking or responding to normal stimuli. It would be best if you go home and return tomorrow. We need to wait and see what transpires."

I paced our bedroom floor back home, speaking out loud to Spirit. "Why does life have to be so hard?" I did not expect an answer; it wasn't a question. I was saying, "When is enough pain enough?" Our first anniversary had been only four days ago. When I saw Mark the next day, his eyes were closed. He did not move, and he could not see or speak. Many medical devices were attached to him, monitoring his body. IVs were attached to both arms, and multiple drugs controlled his bodily functions.

A physician showed me the MRI of Mark's brain and explained, "When we inserted the wire into the aorta, it disrupted deposits on its walls. The deposits went into the bloodstream and circulated into the body. The many white specks you see are blocking blood vessels; every speck is a small stroke. People can recover from strokes, but we don't know what that many will do to him."

Each day I watched and waited for signs of recovery, wanting to see his smiling eyes and hear him laugh again. I hoped he could hear my words and be aware I was there with him. I searched for things to say or do that might lift his spirits and encourage him. He had written delightful short stories about his fishing adventures. I brought them to his hospital room and read them out loud. I talked and sang to him, and felt sure I could see some response in his minor movements. At times a finger seemed to move slightly, or his brow would move. One day I told him I needed to go home for a short while. He made a tremendous, anguished effort to speak. It sounded like, "Home."

"I hear you, Mark, I hear you. There is nothing I would like more than to take you home, but right now, your body can't make it on its own. If they unhook you from these machines, you could die. Please rest." I remembered his saying before we left home, "This could bankrupt us." Trying to ease his mind so he could heal, I said, "Mark, don't worry about anything; don't worry about money. I have applied for medical financial assistance. We will be fine. Don't put any pressure on yourself. Just rest and recover, be at peace."

Friends and family came to talk to him, leaving gifts for him to entertain himself during convalescence. Day after day, he endured tubes down his nose and throat; his arms had bruises from IVs. He was covered with medical apparatuses, and I feared I might bump something that would hurt him. I said to a nurse, "I wish I could hug him."

"It's OK, you can."

Gently I knelt over the hospital bed and placed my head near his, carefully holding his shoulders. "I love you, Mark."

Nine horrible days of suffering passed, and then Mark's body refused to digest the IV foods, so they put him on life support. Brain fog and unbelief dulled my mind as hospital staff told me he no longer had brain activity and asked for my decision. I stood by his bedside and explained, "Mark, I am doing what you asked me to do. I am honoring your wish not to be on life support. If God wills, he will restore you. I love you, Mark." I sat in his room wondering if he could see me; he was in the spirit realm now. The day was ending, and the hospital staff asked me to leave. They needed his room for someone else.

※

COMPASSION

At home, reality set in. Mark was gone, and he was not coming back. It was more than I could process. I found myself filled with mind-numbing pain. I realized marrying Mark had not taken away the accumulated pain from the losses of my father, Brock, and Tom. With Mark's death, all the pain resurfaced with a vengeance. I sat on the edge of my bed, crying and beating the bedspread with my fists. I paced the floor, surprised at my anger; in my former losses, grief was dominant. I was not angry at God; I blamed no one; I just resented my circumstances. My patience with loss was gone; I was tired of covering the wounds. I became aware that the relationships were Band-aids that distracted me from inner pain but did not heal it. I wanted to heal the pain and feel whole even when I was not married.

My dreams and desires had been shattered. The entire time Mark was in the hospital, I had been in denial, expecting him to come home with me. Now it was clear that the joys of my new life with him were over. He had experienced horrible suffering and would not benefit from restoring his family farmhouse. It all seemed so unfair. We both had thought our meeting was a gift, a balm of healing for us both. I felt ill equipped to handle this turn of events.

On April 13, 2017, I journaled: "Mark is gone; it has been twenty days now. I am in horrific pain, weeping with a broken and hurting heart. Each one that comes to my door says the same things. 'He was so young. He seemed so healthy. I am shocked. He was so full of life. He was my best friend. You two were so happy.'"

"Father, he was going to be the rest of my life."

Voice within: *Your wounds will heal.*

Tears streamed down my cheeks. "Please don't leave me here in the River House alone, Lord. Without Mark, the river is not so pretty. I don't like this part of my life story; it is so painful. Please do not leave me to my own understanding. I need you."

On April 15, 2017, after twenty-two days without Mark, I wrote in my journal: "Lord, you said you would never leave. Why do I feel so alone? Where is my Mark to walk with me by the river? Where is his hug and kiss to warm my heart? Where is the fruit and tea he brought to me each morning? Where is the joy that bubbled up as laughter and manifested when I played the piano? I feel left. I feel disappointed. Your word says you 'set the solitary in families.' I was back in a family for such a brief moment. It is gone, Lord. There are no eyes to stand next to me and watch the sunrise. There is no arm that wraps around my shoulder. The emptiness is vast." The voice within responded.

> *Eternal truths are the only comfort in the land of the living. To feed on Spirit is the only way to survive and thrive in this world. I am Spirit and I am always with you. You must walk with me by faith. I have said I will never leave you, and I will not. Mark is with me, by my side. He has entered into rest. You must enter a place of rest in your spirit. Your work is not yet done. You have words to write, words to speak, and paintings to paint that will capture the attention of those I reach out to. Be my hands, be my heart. I place within you this day a heart of compassion for those who weep. Words of authority and authenticity as only those who experience can speak. Always let my Spirit flow through you. Do not block my thoughts and words that come into your spirit. I am Spirit and I am life. You are not alone, dear Diana. I will show you how to find comfort. I will be with you, I will hold your hand and watch the sunrise with you. Your heart will not always be empty.*

Mourn for this man that you loved. Allow yourself that. It is love's sorrow. It is not a bad thing. Days of rejoicing lie ahead for you. All is not lost. Mark enriched your life and set you free from heavy chains. He was your friend and your love, yet he was wounded. He now sits in my presence healed and whole. He understands the process. He loves you and you will see him again. You will enjoy him again, but next time there will be no pain, no tears, no jealousy, no sadness. All are one in my father's house. Go in peace, Diana; do the will of the father. His hand is on you for good. Let your hand remain open. Let your lips form praises. Let the music flow, let the art flow, let the love flow. No good thing will God withhold from those that walk uprightly. Streams, streams of mercy flow over you. Joy, joy from the father of lights. Rest my child, rest my Diana. I am Spirit and I am with you.

I had needed the Lord to come, and he did. My perspective changed. Somehow it consoled my spirit to know a heart of compassion had been placed within me. I understood that somehow my loss of Mark had purpose. Jesus said he would be there to watch the sunrise with me, and knowing Mark was healed and whole comforted me.

※

I began compiling a video for Mark's memorial service. First Tom, now Mark—how could this be happening again so soon? In 2014, five years after Tom passed on, I was finally emotionally able to create his memorial albums and video. Only three years had passed since then, and now I was making another memorial video, for my second husband. The nine-minute video was only a tiny peek into his lifetime, but the footage captured his essence. Pictures showed his work with board members and volunteers, planting trees and adding nutrients to the Molalla River to preserve the native fish and ecosystem. I had taken videos of him driving his beloved teal green pickup, restoring his family home, barn, and orchard. I had live scenes of him walking the stream and fly fishing.

About four hundred people attended Mark's memorial service on April

22, 2017. He was sixty-four years old and well known when he died. He had had a unique ability to make a person feel valued. One of his favorite songs, "Don't You Wish It Was True" by John Fogerty, enhanced the video as background music. The lyrics revealed the way Mark wanted the world to be.

> But if tomorrow, everybody under the sun
> Was happy just to live as one, no borders or battles to be won,
> Well if tomorrow, everybody was your friend
> Happiness would never end, Lord, don't you wish it was true.

On my Facebook page I posted this quote by Eleanor Roosevelt, which spoke what my heart wanted to say.

"You gain strength, courage, and confidence by every experience in which you really stop to look fear in the face. You are able to say to yourself, 'I have lived through this horror. I can take the next thing that comes along.' You must do the thing you think you cannot do."

Sedona Soul Adventure

10

Breaking a Pattern

When similar events keep repeating in our lives, we call them patterns. Patterns in relationships are well-known phenomena. When our beliefs change, our responses change, altering our pattern. When Mark died, I recognized I had a pattern: my deepest fear was the fear of being alone and separated from those I loved, and it had been triggered over and over by events in my life. I scanned backward to childhood. There I was as a child, lying in bed, crying and soaking my pillow with tears, feeling pain at thoughts that my parents might die. Then life brought the loss of my father, Brock, and Tom. My response was always the same, copious tears followed by five years of miserable grief. I saw no value in death and grew to hate the pain when people I loved left this earth. Searching for the healing balm became my quest.

Questions filled my mind. What was the purpose of bringing Mark into my life for such a short time? It did not make sense to me. I felt like a baby thrown into an ocean and expected to swim. No training, no warning, swim! I was drowning in new responsibilities, medical debt, painful emotions and thoughts. I did not know what to do with the avalanche of life I was facing. Before Mark, I had kept busy to distract myself from pain. While I was with him, all that old pain had seemed to vanish, but it was a Band-aid covering a wound. Now I wanted to heal and change the pattern. No more Band-aids!

My peace had been negligible since Mark's passing. By reading books in his small metaphysical library I learned that meditation had helped others find peace and purpose. I decided to step outside of my religious corral and find people who taught meditation. Online I found Sedona Soul Adventures (SSA). Sedona, Arizona, is known worldwide for its vortexes of electromagnetic earth energy. Early Indigenous peoples went to Sedona because they felt the vortexes as Spirit energy. Healers gather in Sedona because the energies open spiritual awareness and facilitate healings.

I sent an email inquiry to SSA and received a response from a counselor named Veronika, who told me she would be my angel guide. I discussed my desire to schedule a private retreat, which they called a soul adventure. Veronika scheduled my four-day retreat and chose the practitioners who would help me deal with grief and loss.

✺

During the two-and-a-half-hour drive from the Phoenix airport, a song kept going through my mind. "How could anyone ever tell you you were anything less than beautiful? How could anyone ever tell you you were less than whole?" The lyrics baffled me. Who was the artist singing to? Was she singing to a lover, or was God singing to her? Although I tried to block them out of my mind, the words reached into my heart. As miles of cactus and desert flowed into new scenic wonders, I entered the Sedona area. Awe-inspiring red and gold rock columns towered above the dry terrain. Their presence evoked reverence for creation and this earth. I thought, Surely God made this area so spectacular to make us aware it is a sacred place.

I arrived at the black iron entry gate to my lodging and punched in the passcode. The gate swung open and a one-lane bridge allowed passage over a gentle river and onto a dirt road shaded by a canopy of trees. I followed the winding road to the base of the foothills to find Your Heart's Home, where I would stay for four days. The owner, Ranjita, greeted me, gave me a tour, and invited me to help myself to food. Not wanting to forget any moments of my soul adventure, I began recording in my journal.

"Thursday, July 20, 2017. Dear Mark, I know I would not be in Sedona tonight if I had not met you, married you, and lost you. The music and laughter I found with you are gone from my soul. I don't know what I am supposed to do with my life. I know how to fill the hours with work, but to what end? What am I accomplishing by emptying the house and toolshed of all your things I won't need? Is that my purpose on earth? I found purpose while loving and helping you. Now, all the routines seem so meaningless. Britney is planning on college. Do I belong on the river in a house I can't maintain?"

From my bedroom in the loft, I looked out the windows at the majestic clay-colored peaks. Strolling through the home, I studied the décor. Books, wall plaques, paintings, twinkle lights, crystals, and translucent curtains all spoke a message. Spirit is present here; this is a sacred space. I was not sure what to think of this type of decoration. Ranjita showed me her client room downstairs, containing a massage table with blankets and pillows. The bay window was lined with boxes of oracle cards.

I walked out onto the deck. As the sun sank below the horizon, its rays adorned the clouds. I wondered what lay ahead of me. Would I leave Sedona any different from when I arrived?

※

I awoke to a cool breeze blowing through my open window. A large, perhaps three-foot-long angel figurine hung by a nylon line over my bed. There were paintings hanging on both sides of my bed. On my left was a woman with crystals on her headpiece. Was she a seer? On my right I saw a crystal ball, and a wizard with crystals adorning his robe and headgear. I felt sure that the artwork and ornamentation had deeper meaning than I knew. I wondered what I would learn here. I planned to keep an open mind, expecting that I would recognize what was truth and what was not. I wrote in my journal, "God, heal my heart, give me purpose, and correct any beliefs that need to change so I can have peace."

As I read a pamphlet in my room, *Reflections for Touching Hearts*, one paragraph caught my attention. "Before, I met people hoping to find the love I needed. Now, I find my needs are met just by being a loving being." Britney would be finishing high school and leaving home in less than a year. How would it be possible for me to be a loving being when no one lived in my home to love? How would this be done when I lived alone? My spiritual life informed me and comforted me; however, it did not fill the void left by my husband's passing. In the absence of human companionship, I felt alone, empty, and unneeded.

My SSA orientation was to begin at 9:00 a.m., and I felt great anticipation. From the deck, I looked out over the countryside. In every direction I could see beautiful red rock columns kissed by the morning sunshine. After driving the nine miles of country road leading to town, I arrived at the SSA office. The air was warm as I exited my car. At the top of a small flight of stairs, I entered a glass door to the office. An attractive young blond woman greeted me.

"Good morning! I am Veronika, your angel guide. Come on in, and we will go over your itinerary." She led me into her office and offered me a chair. I immediately liked the seating arrangement. She did not sit behind her desk; we sat in cushioned chairs face to face. She handed me a packet containing pamphlets about fun things to do, local area maps, recommended restaurants, and my itinerary. She ran her finger over the street map, showing me how to find each practitioner's home. I had never pampered myself like this before and was already enjoying it. Asking others for help was a significant leap for me, and I looked forward to what I would learn.

Veronika grew silent and pointed to her right, where a tiny white feather drifted in the air. "It's an omen!" I pondered the concept of an omen and realized I was in the presence of people who did not overlook the synchronicities of life. After the orientation, we walked out of her office to the front desk, where more papers awaited me. Resting by my papers was another tiny white feather. Veronika, two staff members, and I gathered at the counter to observe and ponder this unusual appearance of a little white feather. As I left the office, I prayed, "If those feathers have any meaning for me, please show me what it is."

SESSION ONE

At 10:00 I was to meet Laura for a session on releasing pain and grief. I quickly found the location as it was only a few blocks from the SSA office. Laura came out to greet me and took me into her studio. As I entered the small room, I noticed shelves holding a comprehensive collection of small resin sculptures and bric-a-brac. She invited me to sit on the couch and sat near me on the adjoining couch. A massage table with blankets and pillow was between me and the collection on the wall shelves.

"Why don't you begin by telling me a bit about yourself and why you came to Sedona."

Where do I begin? How much should I share? I did not want to spend too much time doing the talking; I wanted to learn. I followed the prompts of my memory and summarized my story. Grief was surging inside me, and I tried to keep it under control. No one had ever asked me to share my grief. At Mark's memorial service, someone had said to me, "You are our hero." It was then that I realized others were comfortable if I acted strong, so I kept up the performance. Now that Laura had asked me to share, my emotions pushed hard at the floodgates. It was only four months ago that Mark had died. I held back the tears as I told her that I struggled with unresolved grief.

I then took a moment to switch the subject. Fifty-plus years of religious conditioning were not easy for me to set aside. Laura was a total stranger, and I was baring my soul asking for advice. What was her spiritual foundation? Was she in sync with me? Before I came to Sedona, a Christian had asked me, "Diana, why are you going to Sedona? They are all New Age." While I was with Mark, I had already started to question the truth of my religious beliefs. However, my relationship with Jesus was a separate issue. He was not a doctrine. He was a reality in my life, one who had helped me countless times. I needed to know what Laura's spiritual connections were. I asked her, "Do you know Jesus?" She assured me that Jesus was very much a part of her life. I was mildly relieved. I continued, sharing more of my life, and she interspersed recommendations and ways to release grief.

She then invited me over to the bric-a-brac collection. A wooden box filled with white sand sat on a nearby table. She told me to choose items I identified with and place them in the sandbox. My eyes were on a white marble grizzly bear; I put him in the sandbox first. I gathered more items and then looked at my collection in the sandbox, noticing that the bear had a feather glued to its ribcage. My curiosity was growing. Was there significance to these feathers appearing in my life? My choices in the sandbox spoke my heart: I had ignored manufactured items like castles, houses, and cars, and had chosen animals and a symbol of Jesus, a crucifix.

Laura explained that the qualities of each animal might be at work in my life. Each had a spiritual significance. The bear brings power and courage. The horse forges forward in beauty and bravery. The wolf is a companion, a pack-oriented spirit, and the coyote adds humor. The lion and the lamb bring comfort. The mother bird nurtures, and butterflies represent transformation. We left the sandbox and returned to the couch area.

I shared with Laura that at home, after Mark died I had experienced periodic wheezing in my lungs and pain in my lumbar area and left hip. My pain was in the same areas where Mark had begun experiencing body pain about eight months before he died. She suggested that I might be carrying Mark's pain sympathetically and told me I could release it, since I didn't need it and my taking it wasn't doing him any good. I wondered, How am I empowered to do that? Laura said she wanted to do an energy clearing to help me release the pain. I had never heard of energy clearing and was unsure what it meant or how it helped. She then led me in a guided meditation to release the pain. I had no immediate way of knowing if the meditation and energy clearing had been helpful, since the pain was sporadic.

Then we moved to the finale of the session. Laura invited me to lie down on the massage table and placed a soft fabric cover over my eyes. She instructed, "Relax, breathe deeply, and still your thoughts. One of your spirit animals will come to you and guide you on a journey." I thought, Really? I had never had a spirit animal come to me before. She began playing her flute, and I relaxed into the mellow, soothing sound. I focused on the blank, black screen behind my closed eyes.

Spirit greatly surprised me with what came next.

A clear and vivid image appeared, a deep valley surrounded by steep, sloping mountains. Trees covered the slopes from the top of the hills down to what I assumed was a valley floor. I could not see the valley floor; a cloud of fog covered it, filling the entire ravine. Then the ravine vanished, and a snorting, powerful, energetic brown horse was in front of my face. She tossed her head, her black mane whipping the air. Rearing on her hind legs, she breathed heavily, hooves pawing the air; then the hooves came down again, pawing the earth. Her deep, intelligent, penetrating brown eyes looked into mine. It was clear to me that I was to get on her back. The horse had a fearless, authoritative, "Let's do this now" attitude. Her manner resonated with the message: "Come on, I know what I am doing; we have a place we need to go. Get on."

The next scene followed in rapid succession. We were as one, the horse galloping at full speed to a destination only she knew. The ride was smooth; her flying mane revealed the swiftness of the journey. I felt safe and had no concern about falling off her back. She ran on until she came to an abrupt halt at the edge of a cliff. We were in front of the ravine I had seen earlier. Once again, I saw the tree-covered hills sloping downward into a crevasse. The valley below was of unknown depth and covered by thick white fog. I saw a few treetops, their uppermost branches reaching through the billowy fog blanket.

A calming voice spoke within me, *Don't be afraid.* My concerns about receiving help from the people in Sedona were melting. I continued to sit quietly on the horse's back, looking over the peaceful ravine. Without warning, the horse lunged forward, and we began dropping down into the crevasse. I held on tight to her mane as we descended toward the fog cover. Down, down we went like a feather floats through the air. I was beginning to understand that many helping spirits exist. This horse had shown me how to jump without fear into the new, the unknown. Inside, I felt a release to explore, grow, and learn more about my world.

After my spiritual journey, I lay in quiet contemplation on the padded table. Laura remembered from our earlier conversation that my father's grandmother was Cherokee. She sang a soft worshipful melody in a language stemming

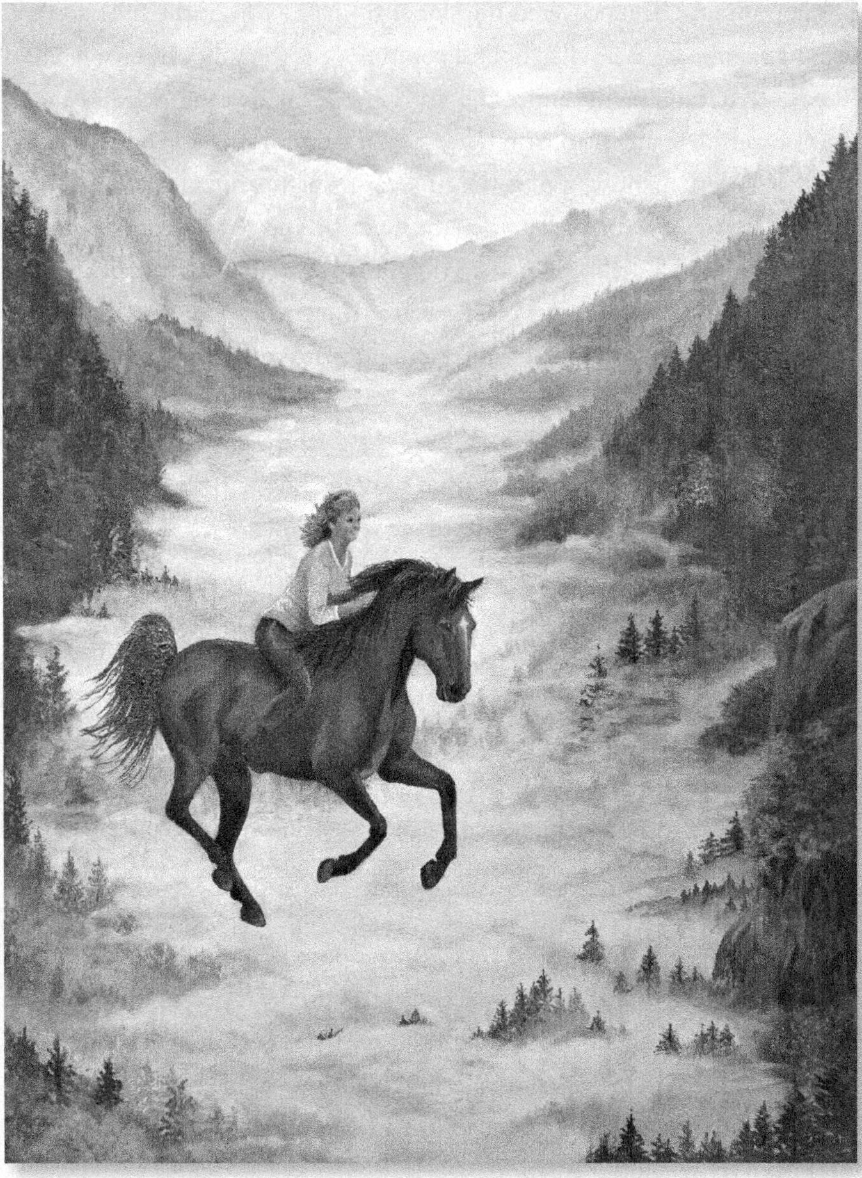

from very ancient Cherokee. The English translation is "I am of the Great Spirit, it is so."

The New Cherokee Morning Song

We n' de ya ho, We n' de ya ho,
We n' de ya, We n' de ya Ho ho ho ho,
He ya ho, He ya ho, Ya ya ya

The melody of the Cherokee song filled the air. I opened my eyes; my session was over. I wondered as I drove away, Will I keep repeating my story over and over to each new practitioner? Today's events were changing my story. I was amazed by the clear visions and messages Spirit had given me in what seemed like the most profound mystical experience I had ever had. It felt like the session had freed me from a lot of fear.

※

SESSION TWO

It was 1:30 p.m. and my next stop was Lisa, who would help me clear and connect through angel therapy. I drove into a subdivision and saw a slim, blond-haired woman outside her home waving me to come her way. Once we were inside, Lisa directed me to the couch and sat on a chair in front of me. After telling me that she would record the session, she asked, "So tell me in a nutshell, what is going on? What are some of the struggles, the who am I, the resistance going on in Diana's world?" I explained that Mark was the fourth major loss in my life and I was feeling fear, anger, and a sense of failure; because my religious beliefs had failed to give me relief, I had come seeking healing.

Lisa summed up my emotions in these words: *rejection and abandonment.* She then asked me if I was distracting myself with joy. This took me by surprise. How could I distract myself with joy when I felt no joy? I sheepishly responded that a to-do list was my distraction.

Lisa told me that she was going to help me see who I was in my own eyes, without my marriage relationships. Her words were breaking new ground in my mind. I had no idea what she meant. She asked me if either Tom or Mark had come to me from the spirit realm. This matter-of-fact question also surprised me, implying as it did that communication with them was a real possibility. I told her no. She then told me that I had a soul connection with them; they were still with me in the spirit form even though they had left the physical form.

She explained what automatic writing and channeling are and asked me if I had ever heard of them. Although I had never heard the term *automatic writing*, what she described was exactly what I had been doing for nearly thirty years. I told her that I knew how to listen to Spirit and record what I heard in my journal. Spirit would speak to me, and I would take dictation. That wisdom and encouragement had guided me most of my life. Affirming that that was exactly what she meant by automatic writing, she told me, "There is a book in you; you will write a channeled book. Once you get the tools and the understanding to reconnect with that divine light inside you, you can then move forward, with grace and peace."

Lisa was making a list of books for me to read, and she added to it three titles by Michael Newton: *Journey of Souls, Destiny of Souls,* and *Life Between Lives.* I felt my deep hunger for knowledge and peace reaching out in anticipation. I told her that I wanted to learn; Mark's death had propelled me out of my rut of trying to find all the answers in the Bible. Spirit had assured me my future was brighter, but I still didn't know why I had such inner pain.

Lisa assured me that the answer was within me, and told me that she would help me get over asking why. She said, "Asking why comes from our ego, our mind. It is mind chatter, old beliefs, things we hear. The mind takes us into that *why* space, why is this happening, why have I lost two spouses, why do I have to struggle, why am I not living my purpose, why? Learn to shift that *why* to the letter *y*, which stands for *yes*. In this shift, Diana, be nurturing and gentle on yourself. Yes, I am having this experience, and while I have it, I am nurturing myself. I am expanding in who I am as a result of having the experience."

I was beginning to understand that perspective, even though it was new to me. Lisa assured me that it was time for me to learn how to receive and told me her own story about needing to learn how to receive. My mindset was shifted by her story, and I realized by not letting others give to me, I was shutting them out, preventing them from giving a gift of love. I could see that I need not call myself a failure. Everyone has times when they struggle. Needing and asking for help is an exercise in learning to receive. She said that I needed to receive from others and from the spirit realm, and that with practice it would get easier.

Lisa paused, listening to Spirit. "You've got lots of angels supporting you, and a powerful guardian angel." She waved her hand. "Whish, he is giving you that nurturing that you need. That's the gift in all of this pain and searching you are experiencing. You are moving toward creative energy, love, joy, happiness, fulfillment, pleasure, and excitement. Find some new things that can enter into Diana's world that you genuinely enjoy doing."

As she spoke, I thought about the singing and the joy that bubbled up in me when I painted. I told Lisa about the times Spirit had told me, *Paint, your future lies there*, and the distant memory of a prophet's words: *Your writing will bring healing to others.*

Lisa affirmed, "Only you, Diana, can access and tap into the creative energy that is true for you. They are showing me more; it is almost like you have suppressed your creative energy, the teacher part of you. As you embrace your gifts, you will start sharing them; we need to teach what we learn. You are compassionate, a nurturer, caretaker; now the shift is toward taking care of yourself. Now you are owning the essence of that love. If you find fulfillment in sitting and writing for ten hours, do it. Nurturing yourself is the heart of what you are learning."

She continued, "Pay attention to your feelings. Observe the energy running through you; is this negative or positive? Am I loving doing this, or am I in negativity and fear? God wants you to be happy, to have joy and bliss. Yes, you have gone through some pits. You are taking responsibility and finding your way out. You are taking action to heal; that is the gift in you. Fantastic, phenomenal!"

Lisa paused again, listening within, and told me, "You are very much a healer by just showing up with your presence." She told me that the spirit world uses four spiritual senses to communicate with us: inner feeling or clairsentience, inner knowing or claircognizance, inner seeing or clairvoyance, and inner hearing or clairaudience. She asked what my strongest sense was and I told her inner knowing; I know what I am supposed to do. Second is the voice within, hearing from my heart, not my mind. Third is seeing, like the vision I had had of Mark soon after we first met online.

Lisa affirmed that Spirit was guiding me and encouraged me to release wanting to move forward more quickly. She assured me that everything was happening in perfect, divine timing, as I let go of the past one step at a time. "It is about where you are right now. The gift is in the present moment." I began to understand what she meant by staying in the moment. Thinking about going to the beach alone would make me sad. I needed to quit mentally projecting myself into the future.

She then asked for the angels to assist me in doing some automatic writing so that I could receive a message from Spirit. As she gave me instructions, Spirit's words were already flowing into my mind. I chuckled with joy because the words were comforting. I was on familiar ground. I wrote the message and handed the paper to Lisa, and she read it out loud.

> *Let it all go, the preconceived, the taught, the ridicule, the fear. I alone know the path you need to walk. There is no other that can guide as I do. Don't fear the new, don't fear the different, and don't fear the unknown. All is known to me, and I am the guide. You know me, and you know me well. Rest in this journey of healing. You will learn what you need to know. —Jesus*

Lisa said the message gave her goosebumps, and then picked up a deck of oracle cards, explaining that they were another way to receive messages. She shuffled the deck, and I drew a card. The message was about my home: angels were protecting it and I was to relax and enjoy my home because all was well. Oracle cards were new to me, and I was surprised at this card's relevance. I told Lisa that I had been fluctuating between thinking I should keep the River House and believing that I should move. Spirit's last word had been to stay. Lisa gave an emphatic, "So stay!" I drove away from her home with increased hope and anticipation.

※

I returned to my lodging, relaxed in the peace of the living room, and watched the crystals sparkling with light from the setting sun. I was beginning to regard rocks, trees, birds, air, earth, and water with new respect for their energetic intelligence. I now knew that the room decorations were tools to quiet the mind and cause it to focus on Spirit. My spirit was stirring, and I recorded a message in my journal:

> *Open your eyes. I am everywhere, in the majestic mountain formations that dazzle your eyes or in the sparkling crystals that hold mystery. Let me freely run through your spirit; we are one. You have the mind of Christ even as the scriptures teach. Trust and do not doubt. Love and do not fear. Do not block the messages by fearing your ego. Let the bread of heaven sprinkle down on you and nourish your soul.*

Sedona was indeed a place where the spirit realm was far more accessible than I had known. I ventured a request that came from deep longing within. Mark had told me that I could hear from loved ones in the same way that I heard from Jesus. I journaled my prayer, "Lord, let me hear from Mark. Let me hear what he would say." Immediately three words came into my heart. That was my signal; I was about to receive. I took my pen and wrote the words that flowed into my mind.

> *I would tell you that I will love you for eternity. I see now the great gift of love that you gave me. I was blind to your sacrifice and selfish in my demands. My heart and soul began healing in the presence of your sincere love. I am in a realm of pure bliss, and I pray for you daily. My darling Diana, I never told you while I was with you how much you meant to me, how much you blessed me. Pure sacrifice and pure love, when I returned cruelty at times. Forgive me, dear one. I*

did not see; I did not know. I was blinded by pain and confusion. I see now; I rejoice now. Be at peace, my love; yes, you are my love both now and forever. I will not stop loving you. —Mark

Tears flowed from my eyes as his loving words touched my heart. Somehow, he now knew how much I loved him and how much I had left unsaid. Somehow he now understood the pain that his words had inflicted. During our short time together, I had overlooked his blindness, believing that in time he would heal and recover from the injuries he had suffered in his life. I never shared those thoughts with him; I just kept loving him. Now, somehow, he knew what I had felt. In David Sunfellow's book, *Love the Person You're With,* I had read case histories of people who had had near-death experiences. They had seen their life review and witnessed how their words and deeds had impacted others. I thought, Mark must have had his life review. It was healing to hear him speak. I was delighted. I had heard from Mark! Four long months had passed since his transition to the spirit realm.

The song I had heard within on my way from the airport persisted in my mind: "How could anyone ever tell you you were anything less than beautiful? How could anyone ever tell you you were less than whole?" I kept rejecting the song's intrusion, thinking I did not need this message. But it would not stop, so I paused to think, Is this a message from Spirit? This song speaks of beauty, of not letting anyone say you are less than whole. Am I burying some pain of rejection? Am I telling me that I am less than whole? I spoke the lyrics out loud, using them to nurture my soul. "I am whole, I am loved, and I am beautiful." I went to bed with a happier heart.

11

Paradigm Shift

I woke with expectation on day two of my adventure. Sedona's buzzwords for the invisible realm filled my mind: *energy, chakras, spirit guides, reincarnation, meditation, visions, omens, the third eye*. It was almost 10:00 a.m. when I arrived in a nicely landscaped subdivision with attractive stucco homes. A lovely white-haired woman stood on the sidewalk, directing me where to park my car. Sher was beautiful; her countenance glowed, as I might expect of someone who specialized in radiant heart healing. She led me to a private room, a sanctuary of soft sunlight, soft colors, and a comfortably cool temperature. We sat down on cushioned chairs, face to face, like friends.

"Tell me your story and your reasons for seeking my help." I briefly described my needs, and then she told me about her background. She had a doctorate in clinical psychology and had founded holistic health care programs. Her focus now was helping people connect to the energy of their souls through a method she had developed called radiant heart therapy. She explained, "Since I began this work, I have seen rapid transformation and healing in clients. I rarely use my clinical training in psychotherapy anymore. Energy healing is more effective. When people focus on the soul level, they heal more quickly."

She had me lie on her massage table, where she would check the energy levels of my chakras to identify those that needed attention. At the end of the session, she would recheck to see what changes had taken place. I looked up into Sher's serene face. She was on my right, holding a crystal pendulum above my root chakra. "This is not good; look at the crystal."

I raised my head and looked down at the pendulum. It hung lifeless, without motion. I asked, "What does it mean?"

"Your root chakra is closed, indicating no will to live."

Her report surprised me, but I thought I knew why that chakra was closed. I explained how I had missed Tom when he died and had read books about heaven, trying to reach him by visualizing our reunion in the spirit realm. While I had dutifully focused on my responsibilities and my daughter's needs, I was also looking forward to my exit from this planet. I had gotten two years of reprieve from the pain of loss when I met and married Mark, but I was back in the same spot again, looking for a way to get to heaven. I was not suicidal; I just wanted relief.

"You have to stop that," said Sher. "It is known as a death wish, and it will kill you."

She moved the crystal pendulum up the centerline of my body. "Your power center, the third chakra, is open." At the fourth chakra, the heart center, she paused. "It is as I thought; your heart chakra is closed."

"What does that mean?" I asked. She looked me in the eye. "It means you will not attract people to you who will love you. You have closed off your energy in that area. You need heart healing; you need that energy to flow again. That is what we are going to do today."

She moved the crystal again, this time hovering over my throat, then my forehead, and finally my crown. I was relieved to learn these last three chakras were strong and healthy. She told me they were my spiritual connections. I mentally connected the dots. For most of my life, I had nurtured my spiritual connection daily, and that was why those chakras were strong.

Sher gave me this affirmation to repeat daily: "I'll do whatever it takes, as long as it takes, to heal my grief and come to peace about both deaths."

We went back to the couch, and Sher sat next to me this time. She began with prayer, inviting a host of helping spirits to aid in my healing. I was noticing that all the healers invited angels, spirit guides, and ascended masters. It was nice to learn there are so many helping spirits. My perception of the spirit realm was expanding.

"Radiant heart therapy helps people open their hearts to the spiritual energy of divine love," Sher explained. "When you become conscious of your energetic connection to your soul, you connect to your inner child, divine love, and other human beings. The heart chakra opens when you have a radiant heart, and you experience peace, joy, and love. This radiance is our natural state of being; it is the beauty of our soul energy. A person with a radiant heart is conscious of their soul path and finds fulfillment in life through following that path."

It sounded wonderful to me. She explained that thoughts and emotions are energy and that unresolved pain creates blocks and can result in disease. The trauma and negative thought patterns in my life had created energy blocks. Additionally, I had believed that grieving was in some way not accepting God's will. Scriptures in the Bible had reinforced my way of thinking. Having read "in everything give thanks" and "rejoice in all things," I had thought I should not tarry too long in my losses. Now I was learning that the suppression of painful emotions is what causes energy blocks, which manifest in the body as physical and mental pain as well as disease.

The good news I was learning was that I had creative power. Because my consciousness created the energy field within me, I had the power to transform my energy field through my thoughts and facilitate my healing. Intention and visualization were creative actions I could use to alter the energy in my body. My thoughts and soul energy could clear the blocks in my body and open my heart chakra again. Using the mind, will, and imagination were tools Sher would teach me to use to bring needed changes.

As we sat side by side on the couch, Sher asked, "What is it that you want? What do you hope to receive?"

My answer was immediate: "I want to laugh again, real laughter." Grief rushed into my throat as I spoke. "I have been putting a smile on my face, but laughter is not in my heart."

She asked me to close my eyes and instructed me to visualize a dark ball within my chest that would serve as a holding place for the pain. "Now, use your imagination to move the negative energy into the dark ball." I saw the negative energy moving like jagged red and blue forks of lightning into the dark ball. "Now, send four strong roots from your root chakra, located at the base of your spine, down to the earth's red core." I watched big thick roots burrow into the earth and connect to the earth's core. She told me to invite my cells to vibrate in sync with the energy of earth. "Feel the earth energy open your heart chakra and repeat, 'I am grounded to the earth, I am grounded to the earth.'" I repeated, "I am grounded to the earth."

Sher then said to visualize a silvery ball of radiant spiritual healing energy high in the universe. Following her guiding voice, I opened my crown to the radiant energy; it flowed down my spine, balancing all my chakras. I saw the red earth energy and the radiant healing energy merge and swirl together in my heart chakra, as she instructed. I visualized radiant light filling my heart and entire body, displacing the dark ball of negative energy. Sher's hands were warm, one on my back and the other over my heart. Her presence was angelic and comforting. She felt like a friend I had known for a lifetime.

There was more to come. Even before Sher told me to open my crown chakra, my inner vision gazed upward through a portal above my head, and I saw blue sky and white clouds. I could see an armored, muscular man kneeling on a foundation of some kind, one knee up, the other down, as if he were kneeling and reaching into a river. His focus was on his moving hands, which were working at something I could not see. I told Sher, "I hear a message: *Be whole.*" She had a pad of paper and was writing down everything I saw or heard. We both shared when we understood what the images meant.

I watched the negative energy leave my body and the red and silver energy fill my chest. Then a series of images began. First came a dove, and the message of peace. Following that came a bright white light far off in the distance. It was the tiny figure of a man clothed in a long white robe. I hoped it was Jesus and wanted him to come closer. Too quickly, the scene changed. I told Sher, "I see a woman with her face turned away; she is not looking at me." Sher told me, "That is you; it is the way you have treated yourself. You have

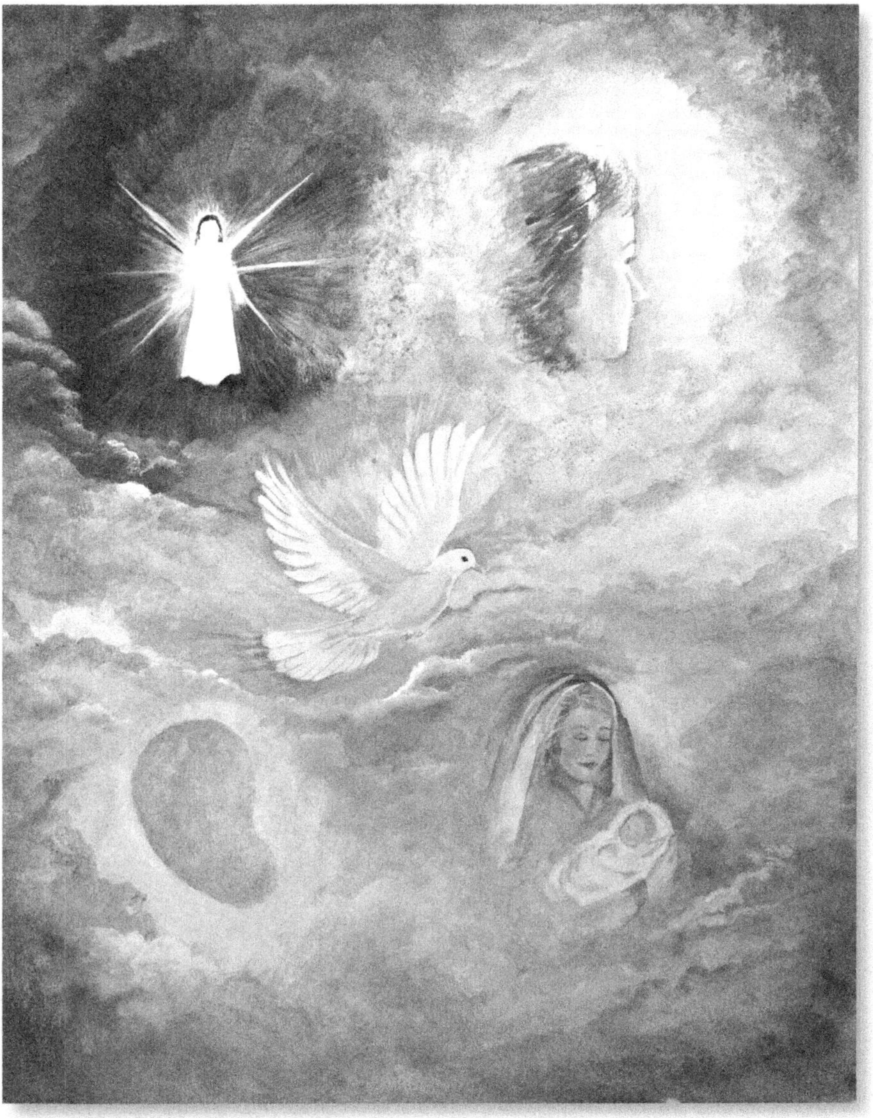

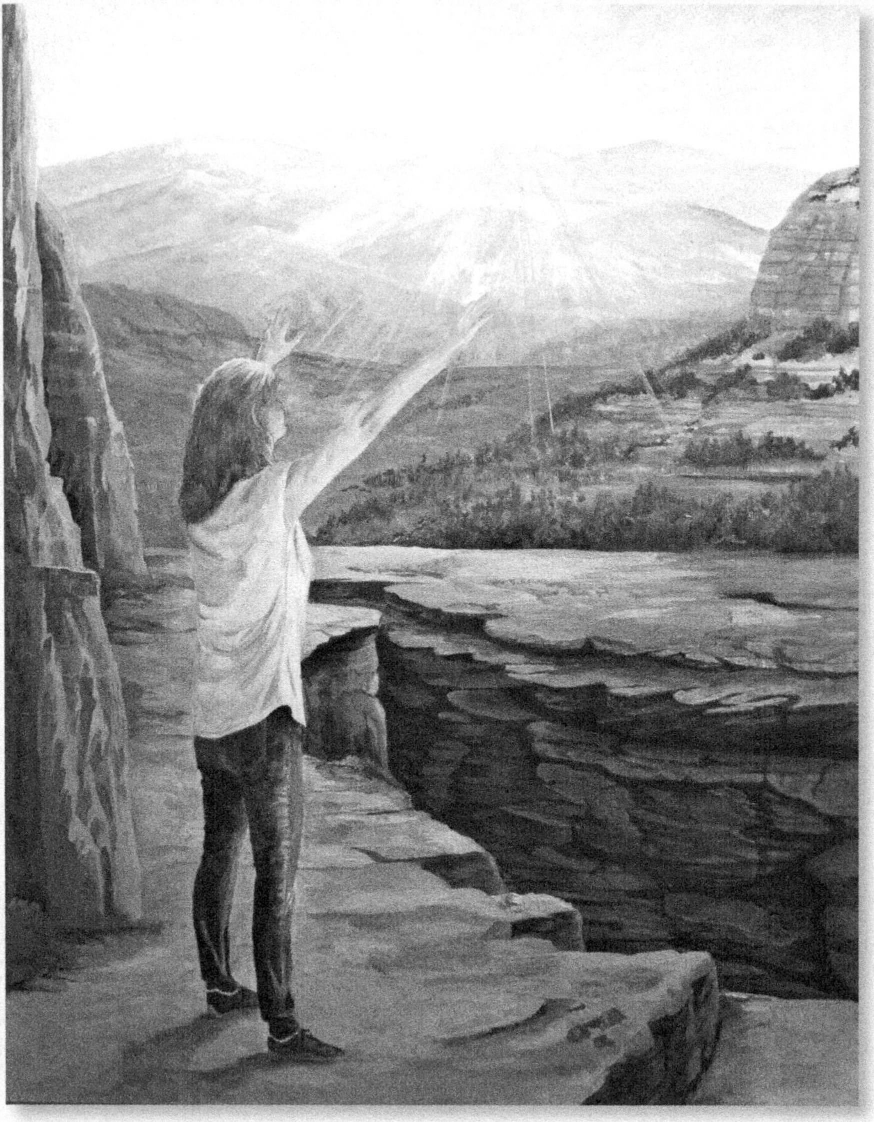

not been looking out for yourself. Now is the time to focus on you." Within the swirling golden clouds I saw what appeared to be a womb with a pear-shaped form developing within. A woman appeared wearing a blue shawl and holding an infant. The message in the images became clear to me. I was the baby in the womb, and then I was in the mother's arms. I understood that a new me, like a new birth, was emerging from this process. Jesus and the dove of peace had overseen all that was taking place.

Next I saw the ravine I had seen the day before during my session, only this time there was a soft tan dirt trail. I was standing on the path wearing jeans, a t-shirt, and hiking shoes. Sunshine bathed the expansive panorama of mountain ranges before me. My worldview and understanding of life had expanded. My arms stretched upward and outward, welcoming the entire world and giving thanks. I had been rebirthed and grounded once again to mother earth. I felt excitement and the will to live. Spirit was filling me up with the desire to stay on this earth and finish my course. A warm joy was returning, removing the aloneness, emptiness, and lack of purpose. I opened my eyes, knowing I was never going to be the same. We thanked God and those in the spirit realm who had helped me.

※

Sher and I sat on the couch talking. I told her that I had sold or given away many things that were precious to me during my time with Mark. There were gifts from Tom, exceptional furniture, objects that held sweet memories, the collection of my lifetime. Mark had distinct tastes and did not gravitate to what I owned. I thought I needed to leave my past behind to merge with Mark's lifestyle. I felt some pain but dismissed my feelings, reasoning that harmony in marriage was the priority. I believed that a good relationship would compensate for the loss of my precious things. However, I now realized that I had given up too much. My things were a part of me; I gave up myself to fit into another person's world.

Sher told me a story about a man who had lived his life to please his wife. He wanted to be an elected official, and in his job he was in a position where he could achieve that dream. But his wife threatened to leave him if he got elected, so he gave up his job and his desires. Eventually he became ill with cancer and died. Sher warned me that giving up myself for the sake of somebody else was the first step down the path to the death wish. "It might have killed you if Mark had continued to live. You were giving up yourself for his sake. Living to please others and sacrificing yourself for their desires and dreams is deadly to your own life and person. It brings disease."

She paused and went on to say, "I believe there is a book in you. What we receive, we are meant to share." She moved her hand as though holding a pen and wrote on an invisible paper within an invisible book. She closed the invisible book and handed it to me, showing me how simple it was to write my story and pass the book to others. She was the third practitioner in two days to tell me that. I had never thought about sharing my life experiences; it had never occurred to me that what had helped me might help others.

We returned to the massage table. Sher held the pendulum of crystals over my root chakra and it began spinning clockwise. The desire to live had returned. She informed me that I was grounded to earth again. I asked her if she was a shaman, and she said yes. Somewhere in my history, I had added shamans to my list of beings that a Christian was not supposed to associate with or listen to. But here was Sher, who was a wise, beautiful, well-educated woman who had just helped me find healing. She knew Jesus, and my entire experience with her was Spirit-led. I could feel my paradigm shifting.

I asked her, "How will I know my purpose?" She answered, "Your purpose right now is to facilitate your own healing." I told her I would have to learn to focus on myself; I didn't know how to do that yet. My focus had been on helping others, pleasing them, and that process had given me a sense of purpose. It had not occurred to me that it was essential to take care of me first.

Sher looked down at me lying on the table and said, "You were probably a monk or highly spiritual being in a previous life that needed this experience of taking care of your own soul." I followed up on her comment about a previous life, telling her "I don't know what to believe about reincarnation." She said she did not believe in it either at first and recommended I read two books, both by psychiatrists: *Many Lives, Many Masters* by Dr. Brian Weiss and

Twenty Cases Suggestive of Reincarnation by Dr. Ian Stevenson. She rechecked all my chakras and found they were happily spinning with energy. We hugged goodbye. I left her home changed; I was not the same person who had come to Sedona. Hope, gratefulness, and joy flooded my being.

※

SESSION FOUR

At 2:00 p.m., Kenyon met me outside her home for my session with her, described in my itinerary as emotional clearing through body wisdom. In the entrance hall of her house, I noticed a painting on the wall and said to her, "I am beginning to understand why there are so many blurry paintings in Sedona. They are like what I have seen during my sessions." She smiled and chuckled, repeating my words, "blurry images." We entered her living room and sat down on comfortable chairs. I shared my reasons for coming on a soul adventure. She started swatting her hand across her right ear as though she were batting a fly away. She informed me, "Someone is trying to help you."

At that moment, I saw a translucent flash of Mark's outline beside her chair. The outline appeared as red and blue neon light. He was standing right where she had been shooing the disturbing presence away. I was amazed, delighted, and laughing as I exclaimed, "It is Mark!" When I saw Mark, I also had a flash of the outline of a tall, quiet being off to my left. It was Tom, my first husband, and I felt honored they were both accompanying me on my retreat.

Kenyon administered her healing gift through reiki, an energy healing technique that uses gentle touch. She led me into a small room and had me lie down on her massage table. My role was to relax and receive. This was my first experience with reiki, and I did not understand the process or the objectives. I observed her as she held my feet, intently tuning in to energies and Spirit. She said that the energy of my feet revealed something was not quite right and asked about my relationship with my mother. I told her I had not bonded with my mother in my youth. It surprised me that she could energetically detect my disconnect from mother. She placed her hand under my back for a while, then positioned herself by my right side and moved my knee and thigh using pressure from the palm of her hand. She continued focusing and working while touching my body with her hands. Because receiving was something I had very little practice in, it was difficult for me to turn off my mind and relax.

As she worked, I talked. I kept thinking I should quit talking and focus on feeling or sensing what might be happening during the treatment. However, I could not seem to stop myself from talking. She focused on her work and let me talk, interjecting a few comments and periodically responding to my questions. She explained one thing about pain messages in our bodies: "If you have pain on the right side of your body, it comes from trying to look into the future. Pain on your left side is due to looking back."

That certainly matched my experience. I began noticing severe pain in my left hip the month after Mark died, and of course, I was looking back. Kenyon instructed me to live in the moment, focus on taking care of myself, and not sacrifice myself for others. I told her how my father and my younger brother had both sacrificed themselves for the sake of others. When they got sick and could not contribute, they saw themselves as a burden to their family. Their beliefs led them to sacrifice their well-being and had contributed to their deaths. Kenyon heard an inner message from Spirit and told me, "This pattern of sacrificing self is a strong reoccurrence in your family." She continued her energy work. I lay on the table thinking that I did not want to continue the family trait; I did not want to sacrifice myself anymore.

As she continued to administer reiki healing energy, she told me many of the same things others had said since my retreat began. I knew that repetition is one of the ways Spirit speaks to us. Every practitioner was giving me the same message: now is your time to nurture yourself. You are not to sacrifice yourself for others. You are to be gentle with yourself, build yourself up, and then use your gifts to help others.

After the reiki session, Kenyon shared her thoughts with me. "There is a book in you. You are way beyond most people and have a direct line to Spirit. Use your gift and write for the benefit of others and yourself. I would like to read it when you are finished." Where had I heard that before?! She recommended that I go to Whole Foods and buy walnut essential oil, manufactured by Bach, to help me stay focused in the now and not look backward or forward. She told me that arnica gel could help relieve the pain in my low back and legs. I left feeling grateful for her work and words, and delighted that Mark and Tom had shown themselves.

※

Back in my room, I opened my journal and prayed for a message from Spirit.

> *You have had a long day and a strenuous spiritual journey into new territory. I am pleased with your surrender. Your body and soul are healing. We are all working with you at your request. Don't be afraid, darling Diana; we are with you. Rest tonight and let the dreams do their work.*

12

Breathwork and Journey

The veil between the spirit and earth realms is thinner in Sedona, and I wanted to use it to my advantage. Early in the morning of my third day there, July 23, I decided to see if I could talk to Tom. I inwardly reached out and thanked him for all the years of kindness he had shared with me. The voice within responded, and I recorded in my journal: *You were there for me too. You inspired me to value myself. You gave of your life to help me fulfill my dreams. I, too, am with you in your journey. I love you, Diana.* I was so grateful to have this experience of communication with him. I knew that other cultures, Indigenous tribes, and Native Americans had long believed that deceased elders and family members are right here with us. They honored them and called on them for wisdom. Now this understanding was my reality too.

A little later, I felt the unmistakable moving of Spirit within me and knew there was more to come. I wrote the message in my journal:

> *Write, write what I say. I am beginning a new chapter in your life. It is called evolution. You are understanding your calling and your purpose. You are knowing that you are valuable and therefore worthy of your own nurturing. Nurture your soul as you sit at my feet. Nurture your soul as you show kindness to yourself. Nothing is by accident. All of life is a tapestry, a weaving that is orchestrated by my hands. There is so much more, dear Diana, my little daughter who sits at my feet.*

I see your heart, it is pure, even as you requested it to be. Years ago, when you cried out to me for a pure heart, you and I both know it was given. You have walked in this awareness that you no longer desired the evil that draws others to their death. The unclean, the foolish have no grip on your soul. You delight in the works of my hands and trust me as your source. It is the great I AM that has given you this. It was the desire of your heart and it is done. Blessed are the pure in heart for they shall see God. That is what you asked for, and that is what was given. Go in this strength, that I AM with you. Your guide, your love, your God.

I was excited to see what this day would bring. My first two days in Sedona, I had learned and experienced far more than I had expected to. I had new objectives, new visions, and new goals. I understood that self-nurture was not selfish; it was essential to my future, health, and contribution to life and others. I had learned why I had had such a difficult struggle when my husbands died. It was because I had never learned to love myself but had survived on their love. I had enjoyed serving them, and their gratitude had been nurturing to me. When they died, something in me died. I had lost my purpose and felt no one needed me. It was as if the whistle had blown and the announcer had said, "Game over!" I knew what to do now; I would encourage myself, honor the nudges of my soul, and take time to play. I would find the strength to complete my journey and fulfill my purpose through this.

My awareness had opened to embrace the helping spirits. They had shown me their presence and my value; I was not alone. The concept that all are one was still in the embryo stage of my understanding. Yet, on some level, I got that we are not separate; we are all connected, all one, always. So why should I marvel that I could hear the quiet voices within my spirit?

SESSION FIVE

As I drove to Miguel's home for what was billed as an inner journey with breath and sound, I felt hopeful anticipation. It was the third day of my soul adventure. Would there be more discoveries and breakthroughs in awareness?

Would meditation instruction open more of the spirit realm to me? Warm morning sunshine poured through my car windows as I parked in his narrow driveway. I walked past the carefully manicured green shrubs lining the concrete path. Bright sunlight reflected off the ivory surface of his adobe home. I knocked on the front door and waited in the shade of the overhanging porch. The door opened, and a slender young man with dark hair greeted me with a smile. His voice was soft, his manner peaceful, gentle, and kind. His eyes glowed as though they were reflecting light from some divine inner source.

As he led me toward his client room, I passed framed diplomas displayed on a wall. The many certificates of completion revealed his extensive study of metaphysics and meditation. We entered a quiet, softly lit room; it felt sacred, like a place of prayer. A window shade blocked the bright noonday sun; a flickering candle added to the room's soft glow. On the carpet in front of the couch, I saw a long pad with a head pillow on one end, and I knew Miguel had prepared that space for me. Miguel sat down in a chair and invited me to sit on the couch facing him. We were only a few feet apart. "Tell me what brings you here."

I scanned the past two days of experiences that had altered me. Today, I no longer had a need to talk about loss, grief, or loneliness. The broken me was rising; the allies of insight, excitement, and adventure were helping me to stand up. I was ready to listen, learn, and move forward in life. I gave Miguel a brief overview of my struggle with loss and my desire to learn about meditation. As I shared my story with him, I felt a concern lingering inside me. It came out in one sentence: "I only want the truth."

He was quick to respond, "That is a good goal; the truth is what you will get." He went on to explain what I could expect from meditation. "It is through meditation, being with ourselves, that we make the unconscious and subconscious fully conscious. During meditation, we learn how to experience what is inside of us from a neutral place. We are just experiencing every thought, every fear, every feeling, and going for the ride it takes us on." He told me that during meditation I could jump down the rabbit hole of every fear, worry, or feeling and just be with it. He said I could safely experience each thought or emotion and heal whatever came up as energy. "If you are willing to love whatever is inside of you without fear or judgment, there is never a reason to fear. It is fear that causes us to get busy and distract ourselves. We do anything to avoid facing loneliness. Fear keeps us unconscious."

I was pleased by his responses. He understood the problems of fear, and he had some solutions. His description of using distraction to avoid facing negative emotions was on target for me. He explained that during meditation I could decide to face fear. I could decide to fall in love with being alone. He suspected I might be thinking, I won't be enough entertainment for myself, or I won't have any fun, or I need certain people to bring out these different parts of my personality. He assured me that even those aspects of my personality were just a fragment of who I am. He clarified, "We are talking about learning to truly know thyself. We are talking about a self that is beyond the human personality. Are you aware of that?"

I was in a sobering new world of thoughts, and hope was rising. Miguel knew a path to Spirit that I had not found. I inquired, "I don't understand what you mean about knowing myself beyond my human personality. All this is new to me; I do want to learn how to face and deal with disruptive, negative emotions. I want to experience knowing myself. I never thought about embracing the loneliness; I have avoided it." He responded that most people do avoid negative emotions because it seems logical, but logic is not always wisdom. We resist, defend, and protect when we are in the lower mind of fear. Miguel was giving me new ways to look at life.

He said we come to earth to master ourselves and should not be focused on racing back to heaven. "This earth is where our spiritual evolution is a zillion times greater than being an angel in heaven. It is not challenging in the heavenly state because all is in harmony there; you know who you are. The veil comes down when you come to earth, and you think, oh, I am this human. We then have to face our fears and awaken from that."

He was referring to evolving spiritually through reincarnation. This perspective was so different from what I had learned. Religion had taught me that all humans are unclean sinners who need to repent from their sinfulness, get saved, and do good. Just as Miguel said, I had been focused on the "race back to heaven." If what Miguel was telling me was true, I should be working on mastering myself instead of grieving my losses and longing for heaven. Thinking of life as a series of custom-made experiences providing an opportunity for my spiritual growth was like an elixir compared to my former focus on the fall-and-redemption theory.

His words were like medicine giving me the strength to stay in the land of the living. He elaborated, "To get to know thyself is to get to know the truth. That is what you said you wanted; you want the truth. The truth of who you are is not a fabricated human personality or socially acceptable person in the community." He explained that we need to see ourselves beyond our labels such as wife, daughter, cook, or queen. We need to back up and see who we are from a bigger perspective. We are God's very beloved; we are not our bodies or our thoughts.

Miguel explained, "People suffer because they identify with their thoughts. Thoughts are often what we don't like about ourselves. The wise one knows to question the thoughts: 'God, show me, remind me, who am I really and truly.'" He said experiencing that you are one with God is very different from believing the theory that you are one and the same with God. As he spoke, a hunger to experience what he had was growing in me. He said that when you experience that level of consciousness, it becomes a part of your reality. It makes you unshakeable. You know who you are, and no one can take that from you.

"Meditation helps you work through issues quicker. I acknowledge the level of pain you have gone through. Honor the process; you can learn to go into that place of hurt and be with the feelings; it is a beautiful thing. You won't think, I should be strong and get over this; you can love that part of you that is crying right now. Once that part of you feels totally loved, you start returning to the higher self, the spirit that is always in that state of peace. Diana, you are on a very exciting journey. It is a special time for you; there is a very mystical process happening here."

Miguel's words were a revelation to me. I wanted the unshakeable faith that he had developed and experienced. He spoke not from theory; he knew firsthand. I told him that I had read about what he was saying, and I believed it but had not experienced it. Jesus said, "The kingdom of God is within you." I wanted that kingdom, I wanted the reality of that kingdom, not just a belief that it existed. I wanted the bliss, the peace, the love. That is why I had come to Sedona, to learn what I didn't know. Miguel assured me that pain is a sign, a call to connect, to reclaim your strength. "You will find your strength as you connect with your soul, your true self, the eternal being, made in the image and likeness of God. When you heal, love, and accept everything within you, that is when you genuinely become aligned with your soul."

His enthusiasm was contagious; he was a living, breathing example of one who knew who he was. He spoke of feeling the soul's presence in one's being, following the soul's light and guidance daily rather than acting merely from what we believe. "There is perfect harmony and trust; those things naturally come from the soul. We don't have to strive to be some human ideal of perfection; it is within us. We can call forth our soul and say, come home, remind me, live in here. Remind me who I am, that I am love itself. Remind me of the strength that is within me."

I was encouraged by his joy, the evidence of divine light in his eyes, and the path of wisdom he had just laid out for me. I contemplated his words and wondered about the joys he said I could find. If he had found this place of love and strength, I should be able to find it, too, and he was going to teach me!

✤

Miguel started by showing me techniques and tools to help me relax so I could go deeper in the journey he would take me on. He explained that when we calm the mind, the soul awakens. He told me, "I like to say this session is all about letting go and letting God. Literally, that is all that it is. Just breathing and just letting God guide you on this magical journey beyond the confines of the mind."

The first tool he showed me was breathwork. He explained that deep, rhythmic breathing disengages and anesthetizes the conscious mind, gets energy flowing, and relaxes the body. He demonstrated how to breathe through the mouth, maintaining a steady rhythm and staying loose to find the flow. While I practiced the breathing method with him, trying to mimic what he was doing, he encouraged me to go deeper and put my whole body into it.

This vaulted me entirely out of my comfort zone, requiring me to leave the safety of my reserved persona. I managed to allow myself to make sounds with some ladylike exhales, aware that it did not match his mighty "huh!" on the exhale. I wanted to let go, but my ego was stuck on restrain, afraid I would appear ridiculous puffing out like that. Miguel coached me, "How would God breathe you if you were not trying? Breathe that way; notice the feeling of how God breathes *you*."

I did feel something that was familiar to me, something that would happen when I sought God in prayer. I felt energy tingling in my left hand and saw in my mind's eye a blue sky filled with white clouds. But I was used to being alone when I listened for God's voice. This new environment was making me feel self-conscious. Miguel encouraged me to become aware of the sensations occurring in my heart and to breathe into that area. He said that this was a way to begin using my consciousness as a tool. While my eyes were closed, I was to tune in to what was happening in my body, my inner world, and then to go deeper, asking, What is beyond this? What is the truth of this? What is the truth of who I am?

I was feeling a little like a failure due to the inner battle with my mind. This session was not as easy as the first two days of my soul adventure had been. In those sessions, I had just closed my eyes, and the spirit realm had taken over from there. I saw things and understood messages on those days. This experience was different; I saw nothing, I heard nothing. I was struggling with new terminology and theology as well as the unusual questions Miguel was encouraging me to pose, such as, Who is the knower of this, and who is aware of all this? Those sentences and questions did not flow easily for me. Yet, I was learning a new technique, and I was starting to feel different physically.

Miguel instructed me, "Keep going beyond any mental container that is part of the illusionary construct of what we think God is. Instead, go straight to God on the express route." He continued, "Keep going beyond, keep releasing yourself from any perceived limitation. Release yourself from all hooks, so you are completely untethered. Go straight to God; don't stop. If any old thoughts and fears come in, you can say, 'I don't want, need, or demand anything from this.' Then watch how it loses all power."

We practiced warming up and tuning the chakras. He told me the color for each chakra and then sounded the unique tone for each in a long, slow exhale. I visualized the color and sang with him. Up we went, from the root to the crown chakra, toning each sound, *uh* (red), *oo* (orange), *oh* (yellow), *ah* (green), *eye* (blue), *aye* (indigo), and then the top chakra, *ee* (violet). I felt nothing but peace. Then we stood and swayed and shook our bodies to get the energy flowing. Miguel advised, "Once we feel absolutely amazing on every level imaginable, we are in alignment with God." He showed me one last technique, using applied kinesiology or muscle testing, which involved asking God to move through us and letting ourselves be swayed backward to indicate no and forward to indicate yes.

Next was a prayer of invocation. Miguel led us, pausing after each phrase to allow me time to repeat after him. "I pray, I pray, I pray to God. Please show me and teach me God's wisdom and perspective on the truth of who I am. Help me to love and accept all parts of my humanness, and all other human beings that I have ever known. Take out of me any fear, judgment, or sadness, and replace it with divine love and wisdom to understand all my life experiences and to transcend it. Today I will truly know myself as I am, one with my creator. Amen, amen, amen."

Miguel went on to explain that we were making a space to invite my soul in and to allow the presence of God to live. "Welcome home your soul, the part of you made in the image and likeness of God. It is already one and the same with your creator. Welcome that part of you home; let it fill you up." He paused to allow me time to process what he was saying. My eyes were closed, and I realized that I was still trying way too hard to relax. I had prayed many times with other people in churches, and I prayed at home by myself. In those familiar settings, my mind was on God and not on my thinking. Today, for reasons I could not understand, I was self-conscious and could not focus the way I wanted to. New ideas, phrases, and concepts were trying to find their place in my mind, and my religious conditioning of fifty years wasn't stepping aside politely.

I told Miguel that my mind kept interfering with the process. He coached me to say to my mind, "I don't want, need, or demand anything from this."

He told me not to fight with the thought but simply to be disinterested in it. "Become disinterested in all illusions and call forth the absolute truth of who you are." I momentarily set aside the struggle to understand "my soul" and reverted to my familiar path of seeking divine help. I bowed my head and entered my familiar territory, praying out loud, "Father, I want no illusion; I want only truth. I want to know my purpose; I want to know my calling and service to you. I want to understand my relationship to you in a deeper, infinite way."

Miguel quietly responded, "Amen. So take that beautiful intention into the breathwork ceremony. This is where we truly let go and let God. God will take you on that journey and help you experience all that you need to know, all that you need to feel, and remember all that it is time to remember. So go ahead and get comfortable."

※

I lay down on the mat. Miguel gave me a soft cloth to cover my eyes and a warm blanket for my body. He explained that the music and drumming used for meditation should be loud enough to hear but not so loud it distracted the mind. He said the music would provide a backdrop for my journey and would combine Native American, Eastern Indian, and all kinds of beautiful sounds and tones. He instructed me to relax and focus on breathing deeply. The drumming and music began.

The breathwork journey would last an hour and twenty minutes. My only task was to relax and apply what Miguel had taught me. The music was perfect because my mind was not following it. I began applying the breathing techniques I had just learned. Periodically, I would hear Miguel breathe deeply to encourage me to do the same. Eventually, my mind relaxed, I forgot about Miguel being in the room, and I started seeing images on the black screen of my mind. The scenes changed rapidly, and I viewed places I had never seen before. It was as though I was elevated, hovering over busy marketplaces. Most of the time, based on my vantage point, it seemed like I was about six feet off the ground watching scenes in front of me.

I saw unknown faces looking in my direction; those who looked my way seemed to see me. Some appeared to recognize me, though I did not know them. I saw many scenes of a bustling Asian marketplace; no one there seemed aware that I was watching them. At times I went higher in the air and saw panoramic views of mountains and oceans. I was aware of myself searching for meaning in what I saw. I was not in any one place for very long. I was being moved rapidly from scene to scene. It was similar to watching a video as the scenes came to my inner eye, but it was different because I was hovering over each place rather than being part of the scene on the ground. I was transported to each location without knowing how I got there. Somehow a new vista was instantly before my inner eyes, and I was there. I heard no sounds; I heard no one speak.

The music and drumming switched to closure tempo, and the images faded from my awareness as I once again tuned in to Miguel's presence. Slowly I opened my eyes. Had I dropped into a dream state? There was a definite awareness that I had returned; I had been somewhere, and I was back. Miguel was asking, "What did you experience? What did you see?"

I told him what I had seen and how it had impacted me. The emotion that I felt throughout the journey was consistent with what I was now experiencing in daily life. I wanted answers; I wanted to be informed; I wanted to gain knowledge. It felt like I was searching and searching, looking over the entire world for something that had meaning. It was a reflection of where I was in my life, searching for answers.

I had one more question for Miguel. He had obviously experienced what he taught. I began by explaining, "For me, personal testimony from others carries a lot of weight. I like to know what people experience rather than what they believe. Will you share some of your own experience in meditation?" He shared briefly, but one thing he said rose above everything else he mentioned and stayed in my mind.

"I met Jesus."

I noticed the warmth in his eyes as he recalled that time with Jesus.

As we stood at his doorway saying our goodbyes, I looked again at the unusual glow in his eyes. The peace he had found was evident; he had discovered the truth of who he was. He had met face to face with Jesus, the person I had trusted and called on for fifty years in the most significant relationship of my life. I thanked Miguel and walked toward my car, feeling a hunger to continue this practice.

SESSION SIX

After my meditation workout, I was looking forward to a relaxing massage with Kate at 3:00 p.m. The Sedona sunshine was comforting and warm as I drove the side streets. I found the residence as described on my itinerary, walked down the garden path, and knocked on the door. A young woman opened the door. She said nothing and had a puzzled look on her face. I explained, "I have an appointment for a massage."

Kate softly responded, "You are not my client. My client is sixty-five years old."

"That's me."

Her baffled expression made me smile inwardly. She thought I was too young to be the client she was expecting. When I was in my twenties, I did not enjoy looking underage. As a senior, my attitude about not looking my age had changed. I appreciated that I still had a youthful body and appearance.

Veronika, my SSA angel guide, had suggested that massage was a good interlude between sessions. I had been gifted with some massages in the past but had never scheduled any for myself. Today, I was glad I had listened to Veronika and let her include massage as part of my itinerary. It was relaxing, and Kate gave me some instruction on how to relieve lumbar and left hip pain if it acted up. I left feeling loosened up and pampered. I was taking those necessary steps to heal. Expectation bubbled inside my heart; I still had one more day of my soul adventure.

13

Return to Joy

On Monday, July 24, I woke with anticipation. Today I would meet with Yana for a "spiritual transformation on the land." The instructions were clear: wear hiking boots and bring water. I had been looking forward to this day, as I loved being outside in contact with the earth and nature. As a frequent hiker on Oregon trails, I had seen many evergreens, waterfalls, and rivers. Sedona's landscape was new and exciting terrain. My desire to walk the trails there had begun when I first studied the photos on the SSA website. People were standing on mountain trails surrounded by red and gold rock columns, faces tilted toward the sky, embracing the sunshine and fresh air. I had mentally jumped into those photos, stood on the hillside, and stretched my arms to the sky. Today was my day to revel in nature.

I looked out my window. Oh no! Raindrops covered the glass; dark clouds filled the sky. I saw evidence in all directions that it had rained overnight—wet patio, wet chairs, everything wet. I had envisioned a day of sunshine for my journey on the land. Back in June, when I had shared with a relative who had lived in Arizona that I was going to Sedona for a soul adventure in July, she had expressed concern. "Diana, why are you going to Arizona in July? The temperature is 120 degrees that time of year." Weather.com lists the July average in Sedona as 98 degrees, so I had neglected to pack any rain gear.

As for today's plan, I did not know what to expect, and questions began running through my mind. Should I borrow rain gear from my hostess? Was I going with a group of people? Would they have an umbrella I could use? Soon I realized I should call Yana and get some answers. During the phone call, I learned there was no group; I was the only one going out on the land with her. Yana was my private guide for a hike, a spiritual journey, exclusively for me. We both agreed it was best to flow with what Providence had given; there would be no outdoor hike today. We made a new plan. I would meet her at the SSA office parking lot and follow her car to her home.

※

SESSION SEVEN

Soon I was following Yana's car into the countryside. I was surprised to see little piles of golden and red rock particles that had been washed from sloping hillsides down onto the road. The overnight rain had not been a slight drizzle. We reached her home and entered an expansive living room filled with natural light. The room was beautiful and inviting, with an aura of peace. We removed our shoes and walked across the soft white carpet toward white leather couches. Elegant art and sculpture adorned the room. On one wall was a set of four life-size paintings of goddesses, each representing one of the four elements—water, earth, fire, air.

Our session began with us sitting on Yana's couch facing each other. I explained my reason for coming to Sedona, adding that I had received the peace I sought and now was focusing on discovering what Spirit had planned for me. Our conversation turned into sharing some ways Spirit had guided our lives. It was easy to share with Yana; she had experienced it. Many in Sedona had had mystical experiences; they understood the delights of Spirit synchronicities. I told Yana that I wanted to keep on discovering more about the beautiful realm of Spirit.

Her head bowed, she gazed downward, then raised her eyes to meet mine. "I want to open the doorway and be a mirror for you. This doorway can equip you to own, live, and engage all the gifts you have. You are here to use these gifts in service to others. Your automatic writing is one of those gifts; there is so much that you can bring through from the spirit realm. You can help others; there are so many that are hungry. Many want to crack the window open and find a little bit of this light. You are already in such an expanded state. I work with many different people and recognize that you are in a place where you can be of assistance. You can aid and bring support, solace, and healing to so many people by what you bring through, if that type of service is exciting for you."

"Yes, Yana, it is inspiring to me!" Something was happening; a flame of enthusiasm rose in me as she spoke. My self-view was altering. I had come to Sedona as a grieving widow with no purpose, but now I was beginning to see myself as an artist and a writer. I could visualize that I had something of value to offer to others. The practitioners had modeled service to others. Each one had helped me by using their unique gifts. Their words had breathed new life into me. They had held sacred space for me, enabling Spirit to flow into my awareness.

Yana spoke with a knowing smile, "I know that everything we have ever done in our lives is in line with a higher purpose. There is a setup, an orchestration, a divine hand that has been guiding you step by step by step. Do you know what this next chapter of your life is about?" I was so happy that I had an answer for her question. "I know part of it. Spirit told me two days ago that my next chapter is evolution."

She coached me to pay attention to my emotional guidance. "Wherever there is excitement, whatever draws you, that is how you find your soul's purpose. When you follow what you are passionate about, what you are good at doing, that is the driving force that guides you. You don't need to go somewhere or figure anything out. Every day you take the next step that brings the most excitement and joy."

She went on to explain that my life was wide open; everything was lining up for me, making a path so I could bring my gifts into the world. She described my gift of automatic writing as a tool that could help unclog blockages and open up the creative flow. "Opening up allows divine light, wisdom, and love to pour through you. Then the light flows out through your art and your writing. There is so much that wants to come through you. It will all evolve. Seeds have been planted in you throughout your life; right now, water is causing those seeds to sprout. It has only been four months that Mark is gone; this is a huge step forward for you."

My mind continued to expand as I listened to her evaluation of my life from a spiritual viewpoint. She interpreted all of life as growth and spoke of Tom's and Mark's passings as their gift to me. Because of them, I was experiencing spiritual growth. She said they were my guardians now. I chuckled at that idea and responded, "Wow, I have some good ones."

She laughed, "You certainly do. The minute I saw you, I saw many beings surrounding you that love and adore you and want to support you. Just because we drop our bodies does not mean love stops. They are right here." She told me that her sister, who she was very close to, had passed away and then come to her in two vivid dreams, telling her, "I am not over on the other side somewhere. I am in another dimension that is right here, simultaneous with you all the time. I am just in a dimension that is vibrating at a much higher frequency because I am not encased in this physical form anymore."

My view of life and myself continued to change as Yana spoke words of encouragement. "You are such a pure, beautiful gift, an open channel to yourself and humanity, to the planet. It is time for you now to use your gifts to bring through from Spirit, whether writing or painting or walking; your focus is to do what brings you joy."

I was drinking in this new way of looking at things. It was a balm of revelation for me to think of my losses as gifts designed to assist my spiritual growth. In a backward glance, I saw that loss had been the tool that opened new dimensions to me. My spirit was now rallying to accept life's challenges, and I was learning to believe that there is a gift somewhere in the mix no matter what transpires. It was empowering to hear that my art forms were a gift. Yana indicated that she was hearing from Spirit that my paintings were going to be "transmissions of spirit, wisdom, love, and healing." My spirit responded to her words. I had always wanted to paint under Spirit guidance, with utter abandon.

Yana wanted to draw my attention to the extrasensory perceptions that some think of like a sixth sense. She recapped for me the four avenues of communication from Spirit that Lisa had outlined for me on my first day in Sedona—clairaudience, clairvoyance, clairsentience, and claircognizance—and told me that I had all four. "When you have all four senses, they often merge. You get a knowing that comes with a feeling; you hear audibly, and then a picture comes." She elaborated on clairvoyance, which some cultures call the inner eye, the mystic eye, the spiritual eye, or the third eye. My imagination followed along as she suggested that in the days ahead I might see the spirit realm with my eyes open. As she spoke of the spiritual senses, she clarified how important it was for me to open up and own these channels of communication. She helped me understand that not all people are aware of the extrasensory abilities dormant within themselves.

She encouraged me, "You are a clear, open vessel for divine light, healing, wisdom, love, and creativity to flow through you. It is time for you to step into that now. There is this incredible chapter in your life that is opening up, the path is clear, and you are going to follow it." Again, I was refreshed and inspired by this new evaluation of who I was. It was as though Spirit were telling me repeatedly, you have this bag of jewels. I had not realized until now that the jewels I carried might benefit others.

Yana assured me that being clairsentient gave me a big field of light or aura that others were drawn to. I recalled my ability to read my daughter's energy during her childhood. I was trying to help her understand that what a person thinks or feels sends out vibrations that others can sense. One particular day, she was disgruntled but trying to convince me that she was not. I said to her, "You can't hide negative emotions; people feel it. Your thoughts have energy; your body is sending out negative signals. It feels to me like a porcupine." Yana joined me in laughing at this recollection.

Yana was perceptive, sensing I was in transition regarding what I thought of religious doctrines. She told me she had been raised Catholic and had left that religion because the rules had constricted how she perceived the world. During her three years of work to obtain a masters of divinity degree, she had focused on studying the lost years of Christ. "The Bible has no mention of Jesus from age twelve to age thirty. What happened?" She told me that she had learned from a documentary titled *The Lost Years of Jesus* that he had traveled into India, Nepal, Tibet, and Egypt and had studied with the Essenes and the more esoteric groups of the East. He had brought back five-thousand-year-old Eastern wisdom about energy—about the fact that we are energy, we are light—and the knowledge of chakra energy.

This information about Jesus arrested my attention. If he had respected the sacred knowledge of the East, what had happened over time that had caused East and West to grow so far apart? My mind expanded as I imagined Jesus studying and learning as a man, a human. This information upheld the consistent, unchanging logic of the universe. Wisdom has always been available to all who seek it. It is in the sacred place within all. The universe and all of humanity are one body. Yana emphasized the importance of accepting how my life had unfolded through the churches and religion. "It was all perfect, absolutely perfect because it brought you here. Now that you know, you turn your focus inward, and all the wisdom is here in your heart. You don't need to get it from the outside."

Yana helped me understand more about the chakras. *Chakra* is a Sanskrit word that means vortex or energy center. She reminded me that Christ healed with his hands, and energy comes through our hand chakras. The arches of our feet have chakras; they release negative energy and gather positive energy. "Get your feet on the earth, and develop a relationship with the plants in and outside your home," she advised. "Walk barefoot and connect to earth energy, which is healing, grounding, and energizing." She asked, "Why do you think we talk about chakras? Quite simply, they are the interface between our energy body and our physical body. Each connects to an endocrine gland. When you lost your two beloveds, the trauma of separation shattered your energy field, reverberating to the heart."

I had known next to nothing about chakras before coming to Sedona. As I contemplated her words, I recalled the physical pain and emotional turmoil that began after Mark's death. Now, after three days of chakra and energy work, I felt totally different. What she said made sense. I could feel the restoration, the energy pumping, the excitement to live, the joy.

Yana advised, "Just be gentle with yourself; you have gone through so much. You've got a delicate body; you have a very advanced system. Your body is very refined; it feels things very deeply. Be careful to keep your immune system strong. Do this by allowing joy back into your heart." I was chuckling as I responded to Yana, "This morning when I got up, I felt that energy coming back. The amazing part to me is I feel this even though Mark is gone. I am finding the joy even though I am by myself."

Yana continued, "Every single day in my quiet time in the morning, I start with the crown chakra and open it up. I invite that infinite abundance of divine healing and well-being to flow down like a shaft of light, from the crown to the root chakra. We chose to come to this planet to bring joy into our bodies, so let's be here. We can enjoy walking, dancing, moving, and painting. Every morning open your crown chakra to the invisible realm, pray, and then listen."

This pep talk was tailor-made for me. Her encouragement was washing away doctrines that had made me feel devalued. The paradigm shift gave me peace; now I understood that self-nurture is not self-indulgence.

I remembered the white feather that had started my SSA and was still trying to discover its significance. Yana brought out a deck of oracle cards; each card was an artistic representation of a goddess, each goddess an attribute of the Divine Feminine. I drew a card and turned it over; I had chosen the goddess Wisdom. I smiled as I looked at a female goddess clothed in a gown of white feathers. I was entranced; Wisdom and I had been in a relationship. In the scriptures, Wisdom was referred to as "she." Many times I had asked Wisdom to help me make decisions. Through this card, I learned that Wisdom's name is Sophia. Those white feathers that had shown up repeatedly on my first day in Sedona were Sophia's way of letting me know she accompanied me in my soul adventure. She was responding to the love I had shown her for many years.

Yana smiled and led me toward a side room, saying, "We will go to my magic chair now." I took my place in the white recliner, and Yana covered me with a blanket. The room was cozy and had the feeling of a sacred place. She prayed that our guides and angels would be present to help me receive what they had for me. I closed my eyes as she led me in a guided meditation.

Yana asked me to invite the feminine in. Immediately I saw a woman with brown skin and long black hair combed back into a bun. She was very regal, high above me, wearing a white bare-shoulder gown and glowing with light. I knew this was the one called Sophia. I told Yana what I was seeing, and she told me to ask what gift she had for me. As soon as I asked, the answer came: *peace*. I told Yana, and she prompted me, "Now invite the masculine in. What do you feel? What do they bring? What gift do they have for you?" She alerted me to pay attention to all my senses. I became more aware of my body as well as what I saw, and noticed a feeling of comfort around my heart. I answered, "The gift is comfort."

I watched swirling tan and golden clouds, and a flat, round, golden stone emerging out of the clouds. As I watched the stone, lines were being etched into its surface; the lines depicted the face of a mountain lion. I told Yana what I saw. She asked, "What do you feel?"

"It is fierce."

She instructed, "Ask it to enter and notice where it enters." I was surprised when it entered and told her that it had entered through my feet. Then as I watched, I saw myself once again on a mountain path. I told Yana a mountain lion stood by my side as a companion dog would do. We were traveling the trail together, courage was my companion.

She informed me, "That is your spirit animal. Now, ask your inner child to come." When I asked for my inner child, I was surprised to see a slender, tall, brown-skinned, black-haired woman. She looked Egyptian and wore a gold headpiece and a floor-length kaftan. Yana prompted, "What gift does she bring?" Immediately I heard what the gift was: *meditation*. Then I saw something that began as an ivory flower. The petals unfolded rapidly, and like a fountain, bright colors of light shot out of the center of the flower. Each burst went up higher and higher, like fireworks. I understood that the shooting colors of light represented the revelation that was coming with the gift of meditation.

Yana instructed me to ask if anyone else had a gift. At that moment, I perceived that Mark was there. I saw no physical form with my spirit eyes, but my body felt tremendous emotion. It felt as though he had been waiting for his moment like a racehorse at the gate. He wasted no time but burst into my awareness; this was his chance, his moment to be heard. Tears streamed down my cheeks as I felt his intensity and his earnest desire to comfort my heart and assure me of his love. The gift he brought was comfort and love.

Today was the third time during my four-day soul adventure that I had encountered Mark. His energy was so intense; the emotion flooded my being. I realized that I needed to speak to him so that he would know I understood his message and had received his gift of comfort and love. My face was wet with tears as I responded softly and gently, "I hear you, Mark, I hear you; be at peace." The intense presence softened to a deep calm.

I remained in meditation and once again saw myself walking with the lion by my side on a mountain trail. Green vegetation covered the deep slopes around me. As the lion and I watched the scene before us, the side of the mountain ahead of me transformed into white marble with gold veins. It glistened in the sun like something from a celestial realm. I realized that the spiritual reconnection to those I loved had made my path in this world change into this glistening sacred path. I had hope and courage to finish my journey.

Slowly I opened my eyes. My session was over, and it was time for me to go. Yana and I said our goodbyes, and I headed for my car. Driving away from her home, my soul brought up a song I had been listening to at home on a CD titled *Songs for the Inner Child* before I came on my soul adventure. I had not understood the song at the time. Now the words from the song came up. "It's a joy to get to know you." The happy heart of my inner child was singing. I laughed out loud. This time, I understood; I was hearing my soul. This song came from the one I had unknowingly neglected, my soul, who was now my very dear friend. I rejoiced that I had discovered this companion, and decided I would nurture her and get to know her better.

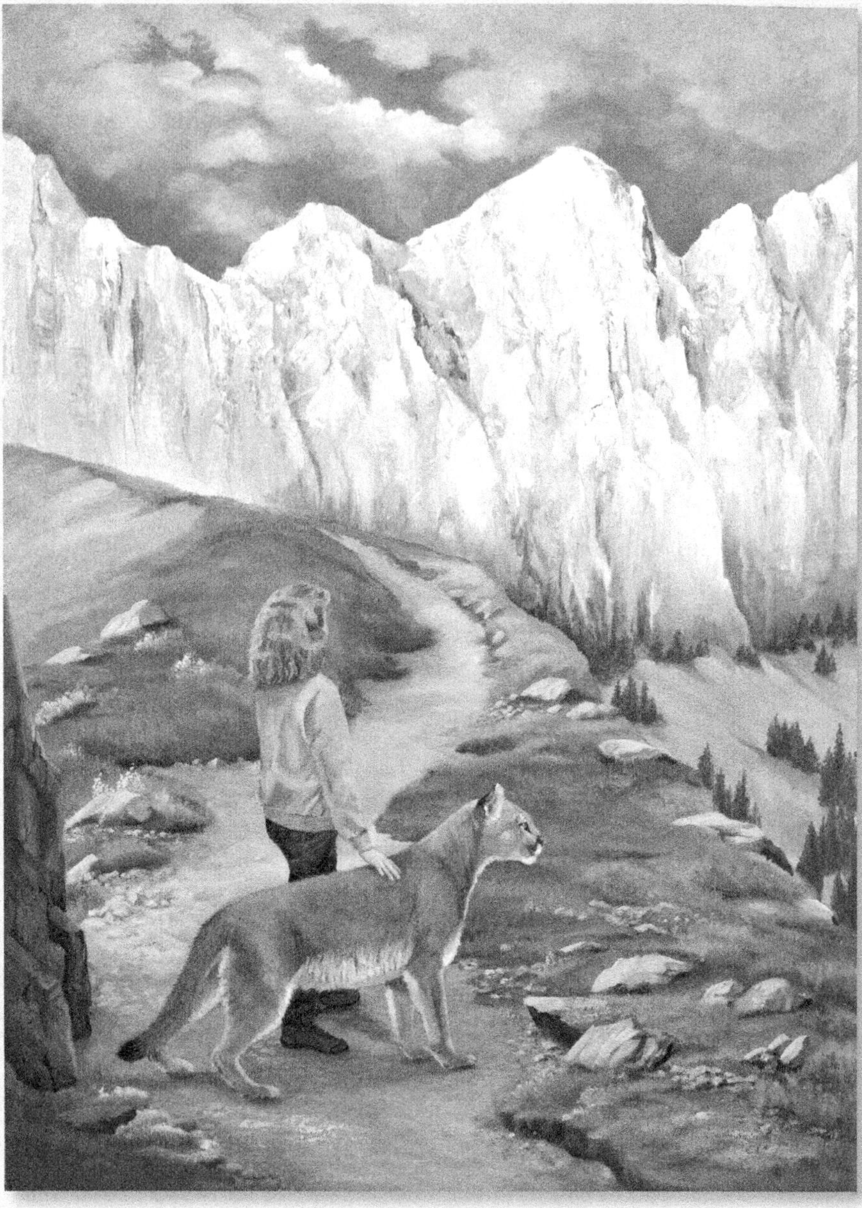

On a whim, I called Veronika, my angel guide, and asked if she could schedule one more session before I left Sedona. I wanted a meeting with Wendybyrd, an artist who painted people's souls. Before my soul adventure, I would never have indulged myself with the gift of a soul portrait. Now, having erased my old script of self-denial, I was following the desire of my heart. I wanted to do something new, something I had never done before, something that seemed fun to me. The soul portrait would be a new beginning, an opportunity to loosen the tight grip of control I had on myself.

Veronika arranged for Wendy and me to meet at Starbucks. We were confident we would quickly identify each other by scanning the crowd. I saw a woman in a khaki-colored hat and thought, *That is the hat of an artist.* Our eyes met, and we waved our hands in greeting. We headed toward each other and sat down on high stools at one of the tables. Our meeting lasted only about fifteen minutes. We talked briefly, sharing what we felt was most pertinent. Then Wendy took the lead and requested that we hold hands and meditate together. Yes, we did meditate right there in Starbucks in front of everybody. After all, this was Sedona, where people meditate in public. Physical touch and meditation were tools Wendy used to access a spiritual connection with her clients.

When our silent meditation concluded, she said, "My, you are just full of animals." She then explained how she would seek guidance from the spirit realm to obtain the details needed to make my soul portrait. She would take notes as Spirit gave her images and messages that represented my soul. From those notes, she would paint a picture that symbolized my soul. She would mail the notes and completed portrait to me. Wendy explained, "Soul paintings reveal things about the spiritual qualities and essence of a person. They are not a physical likeness."

I had that portrait to look forward to. Back at Your Heart's Home, I packed my bags. My Sedona Soul Adventure was complete. Tomorrow I would return home, changed. Spirit had taken over my soul adventure and introduced better ideas into my life. I overflowed with hope and joy because of the abundant love, attention, and instruction I had received. Comfort came from knowing I was not alone, not separate from Mark, Tom, or any I loved. A whole realm of loving, ministering spirits were my companions. I was free to take good care of myself, knowing it was not selfish. Self-care was the best possible way I could help others. I hoped to contribute to Spirit's work. I wanted everyone to know their value and discover this eternal love and support.

I woke on Tuesday, July 25, refreshed and ready to go home. I began with a prayer of thanksgiving. I was grateful for all the ways Spirit had transformed and informed me during the past four days. "I am looking forward to living, loving, and serving again." Spirit responded:

> *Yes, in the day you seek me with all your heart, you will find me. So many other truths have been lost, edited out by the so-called wisdom of men. I remain the source of truth, and I reveal the truth to those who desire it. Seek more, and you will find. I am always with you.*

I left Sedona and arrived at the rental car drop-off in Phoenix. As I was riding the shuttle to the airport, I heard the voice within and wrote in my journal:

> *Don't let your love for me block your future. There is much more for you, total fulfillment, total enlightenment. There is no jealousy where I am. I cheer you on, I love you, I support you. God will supply what you need to fulfill your calling. Keep your spiritual ear close to the heavenly phone. We are on your side, dear one. I am on your side. —Mark*

※

About a month after I returned from Sedona, my soul portrait arrived in a cardboard tube. Wendy had included the twelve pages of handwritten notes she received from Spirit. I glanced through her notes so I could understand the images in the pastel portrait. "Beautiful soul, the light of the creator God pouring into you now. Your spirit is rising; your third eye radiates a brilliant white light; it looks like an angelic being in your sixth chakra. Many beings dance and play in your field. You have a beautiful energy that draws them in! A tree rises from the earth and connects you to all that is. You peer through the branches, merging with it and the earth. Nature is your gift from this world, and you share it through your creative expression."

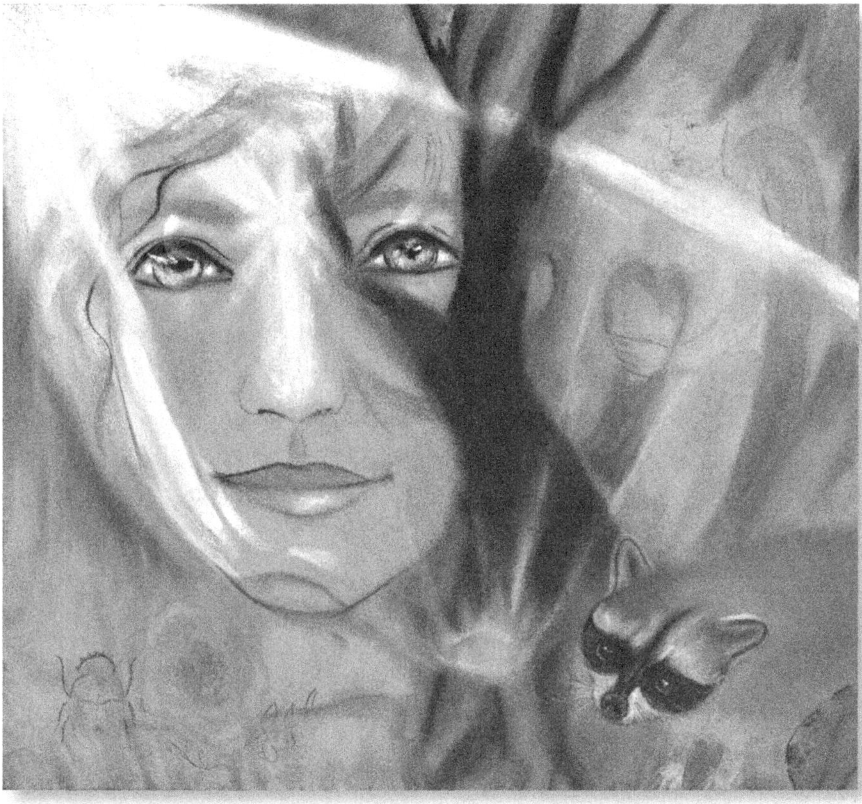

"Everything talks, and your inner ear hears many conversations. You are never alone; you are like the pied piper of the spirit world and this world. A powerful spirit being, a raccoon, appears in your inner world. It is blue-violet in color, symbolic of spiritual gifts and transformation. They have nimble hands, a symbol of yours. Raccoons are resourceful, intelligent, determined, and see in the dark. You have the gift of sight as well; you can see through the veil to the other side. The mask can be your protection; use it when necessary."

When I came to the next part of her notes, I knew she spoke of Mark, and I saw him in the portrait. "An angel rises in your inner world holding a heart. This is a male protector! A love. The vivid green/teal color of the 'high heart' behind him. Behind this being are the aurora borealis in rainbow colors. The sky is alive in color as the morning sun rises, filling you with warmth, inspiration, and light." All was perfect. Wendy did not know Mark or his favorite color, but Mark was in my portrait, surrounded by his favorite color.

Wendy's pages of notes went on to explain every image. The scarab, the pink rose, the sun, all were symbolic and sacred transmissions of love and encouragement from Spirit to me. She ended with, "You are creating a new life with much love and support. Time to hug yourself and fall in love with you."

Back Home

14

Flowing with the Energies

I had come home with new insights and a mindset that had replaced sorrow with joy, purpose, and understanding. Earth had become interesting again. I was eager to explore. Should I stay in the River House or move? Where do I go from here, where do I begin, now what? Britney was making plans for college while enjoying her artistic abilities, her friends, and her beloved cat Harry Pawter, and she would soon be leaving the nest.

My course of action hinged on how I responded to my question about staying or moving. I had conflicting desires. I adored being in nature by the river, but the remote location severely limited my contact with others. I loved the synergy that surfaces with groups and friends, the laughter, inspiration, sharing, and support. Even so, I cringed at the thought of leaving the river, losing the blessings and beauty that only nature can provide. I had to face change and challenge no matter which direction I chose. If I stayed, I faced the daunting task of renovating the River House. Mark with his lifetime of building experience and architectural skills could easily have handled that task, but could I even do this?

My first step in decision making is always to ask, to look for the clues, for any evidence of Spirit guidance. I went back and read the words in my journal dated May 2, 2017, before I went to Sedona. I had been asking Spirit, "Help me know what to do." I heard the voice within say, *Stay, stay in this place where I have placed you, this place you were drawn to. It is not an error that you are here and alone. I am that I AM is with you. I hear your prayer. Be at peace, rest in me.* Sedona had changed me since I asked that question. I would keep moving forward, trusting that I would get clarity about whether I was still to stay. I would know when I needed to know. Spirit would provide clarion inner guidance coupled with clues, coincidences, and synchronicities.

Even if I were to sell the home, I needed to make some improvements and repairs. An architect had designed the house, a one-of-a-kind six-sided, two-level, solid timber home of 2,500 square feet with a steeply pitched metal roof. It was at the confluence of the mainstem and the north fork of the Molalla River, so rivers ran on both sides of the property and were visible from every window. I began adjusting to the fact that the River House was mine. Free from concerns about upsetting Mark, I started rearranging furniture so I could have a river view no matter where I sat, especially from the small nook I had arranged to be my art room. Stepping into the role of decision maker was liberating, and I began to see how beautiful the home could become.

As I sat in prayer and meditation one day, there was a stirring in my spirit. I got my journal and took dictation.

> *Don't move now. The time is not now. What you are doing is perfect, my love; I am so proud of you. I like the way you arranged the living room and the art room. I wish now that I had let you have full rein in being led and being yourself. Wait until you hear the inner voice, "the knowing," dear one. I will be with you every moment. You can be assured of that. I love you as much as you love me.*

Mark's presence was conspicuous! Tears filled my eyes as I wrote the words that flowed into my mind. His message left peace in my heart. When and if I was supposed to move, I would be told; I would know.

✤

I began renovating the River House wall by wall, board by board. The house had been built in 1949, and everything needed repair. I wondered where to start. As if by plan, one by one appliances started failing. First, it was the cold water tank, then the heating system, and on and on. I followed the clues and replaced them. I would wake each morning with a mental download letting me know what the next renovation assignment was. If I didn't know how to do it, I would watch the "See Jane Drill" videos posted on YouTube by journeyman carpenter Leah Bolden demonstrating hundreds of building and restoration techniques.

I stripped off the old wallpaper and tore off scratched, outdated wainscoting. I purchased a miter saw and brad nailer and added new baseboard trim throughout. I patched holes with sheetrock and textured and painted walls. I chose a palette of greens ranging from misty to deep forest, yellow golds from soft to sunshine, and earth tones from brown through ivory. For drama I used Spanish tile red on a few walls. The home came alive with warmth and color.

I hired contractors to install new windows and doors, insulate and sheetrock bare studs, and refinish the wood floors. The exterior transformation was exhilarating as contractors added new sidewalk, river rock wainscoting, front porch pillars, and a wraparound deck. Trained by YouTube videos, I tore off, replaced, caulked, and painted all 280 batten boards by myself, using a scaffold that a woman could assemble.

The former me who thought I could not do it by myself was gone. I was learning self-reliance, how to do things alone without the support of companions. I had always been with others, even during nature outings like beachcombing, hiking, or swimming. To go alone, I had to face the memories of those who were no longer with me. I discovered I could do it, and I did. I developed confidence, physical muscle, and spiritual muscle and added many new carpentry tools and skills to my life.

As I worked on the River House, Spirit was repairing and updating me at the same time. Each event or obstacle compelled me to discover its purpose and value in my spiritual development. I recorded my lessons daily in my journal. I listened to my intuition and the language of my heart, aware that allies in the spirit realm were always there helping me. When I opened my mind and heart to this benevolent help, it came in abundance. Before I went to Sedona, I had addressed only those familiar to my religious group:

Jesus, Father God, and (mother) Holy Spirit. Now I was finding that there are many beyond the veil that desire to help us, that respond when called.

✤

One day in August 2017, just five months after Mark's death, I prayed to meet my spirit guides. Soon the presence of Mark came through, and I recorded these words in my journal:

> *Dearest Diana, I am with you. I have become one of your spirit guides. Don't be afraid. You are doing well, progressing at the pace that you should. Healing is available to you, full healing, body and soul. I love you dear, trust and do not be afraid. We are all growing, it never ends. It is a beautiful plan by our wonderful God.*

Hearing his decision to be my spirit guide was a big surprise. Through the writings of others, like Michael Newton in his book *Journey of Souls*, I had learned that departed souls have many options regarding the continuation of their spiritual growth and that those who leave the earth body are still near to us in the spirit body. I was grateful that Mark had chosen to help me.

He came through with comfort and guidance often during the first year after his departure, like a stabilizing salve that helped me move forward. When I was with close friends, I sometimes shared things Mark had told me. My openness encouraged them to share their encounters with Mark. He had liked to keep in touch with others while he was on earth. Even though he was in the spirit realm, he had not changed. I would respond to the encounters they shared, "Yes, Mark gets around."

One summer day the hot sun beamed down on me as I worked on the exterior of the home, inviting me to go for a swim in the river. I gathered my courage and went down to cool off in the flowing water. It was my first swim alone, without Mark. It was refreshing, but then I remembered how Mark would dive in and pop up in front of me, his smiling face beaming with joy and dripping water. Tears trickled down my face. Later that night, I wrote in my journal, "I miss you, Mark." His response came through the voice within:

I love you, you know. I saw you in the river; I heard your words and saw your tears. Your love for me amazes me. No one has loved me as you have. I love what you are doing to the River House. You are wise, Diana; you have many skills and you are using them well. Trust your heart, trust your desires, and don't judge yourself harshly. Our love was sweet, and it will never die. Love never dies. We will rejoice together in days to come. Be of good cheer, dear one. I love you now and forever.

It was after I learned that spirit guides exist to help us that Mark made his presence known. If my mind had been closed, I no doubt would have missed out on Mark's help. Unbelief, ignorance, ego, and frightening doctrines can erect huge barriers that separate us from divine encounters. After my heart and mind opened, I also heard from Tom, my first husband. He told me how long he had waited to be able to talk to me. All of my encounters with those beyond the veil have come in the form of thought. The words drop into my consciousness when my mind is quiet and I listen with my heart.

�֍

I was learning balance, and the overwhelming number of repairs needed on the house was the perfect trigger for me to work on this. A practitioner had once posed a question to me and offered some wisdom about balance. He asked, "Why do you feel that you must always be doing, doing, doing? When you have low energy, that indicates imbalance. Thinking that you must be doing, doing, is a symptom of wounded masculine energy. You need to focus on your inner house, your self-nurture."

That was good advice, but I was not sure how to follow it. Self-nurture had not been a priority in my life, and it was a new concept to me. My parents had modeled hard work and self-sacrifice. Their example programmed me, and in my marriages, my spouse and family had been my priority. I had found fulfillment through acts of loving service to them. After a life of focusing on pleasing others, I needed to discover what was fun for me. What was play for me? How could I be happy going solo? I did not know the answer to those questions.

I always saw so many things in the home that needed repair. As I worked on one task, my mind was leaping to the next and the next. That split focus created tension that would deplete my energy. I was unsure what to focus on first and sometimes would be working on multiple projects at the same time. Mercifully, I received a message that set me free from the mentality that I was never doing enough or going fast enough. It came during my second year of renovating the River House. I recorded the message in my journal on November 1, 2018.

> *Don't stress, don't be alarmed, rest in each day's moments.*
> *Flow with the energies that move you.*

Inspired words activate the conscious mind and motivate us as no other words can. The words *flow with the energies that move you* ignited my understanding. They were a precise remedy for my problem of not knowing what to focus on first. Those words cleared all the mental and emotional fog out of my way, and I got it. This message helped me begin a new lifestyle of freedom from pressure, the inner whip of life's conditioning to work, work, work every minute. I now understood how to stop the seesaw of trying to do too many things at one time.

I applied this counsel by consciously checking in with my heart to see what I *felt* like doing. I focused on that, dismissing distracting thoughts that tried to pull me off task. When the energy for an activity waned, I checked in with my heart to see what I wanted to do next. It worked like a charm. I had read that living in the moment is a key to peace. Now I was finding a practical way to do that. Seven simple words, *flow with the energies that move you*, became my daily road map. No more self-pressure. Flow when the energy is there; stop when it stops.

It takes a little time to retrain a workaholic like me. So over the next two months, the same message gently came through the voice within, reminding me to keep flowing with the energies that moved me. On November 13, 2018, I recorded in my journal: *You are on track, you are understanding the method. Do not be concerned about the next step. Just take this one.* Another morning, I woke with these words flooding into my mind: *Take it easy, girl, take it easy. You can't get to the end faster that way. The end is not the point; the moment is the point.*

※

Through reading books and watching YouTube videos by Alberto Villoldo, a medical anthropologist who has studied the shamanic healing practices of the Amazon and the Andes for more than thirty years, I became curious about soul retrieval. I learned that life's traumas often cause a portion of who we are to shut down and go into hiding. Shamanism refers to this shutdown as soul loss and recognizes that it can happen when a person collides with hardship, loss, pain, grief, and other unpleasant life events. But we can recover from trauma by addressing it and healing it. In one session, a skilled shaman can discover what might take years for a psychotherapist to uncover.

This led me to schedule a soul retrieval session with Christina Pratt, a highly recommended shamanic healer and founder of the Last Mask Center, with branches in New York and Portland, Oregon. In my soul retrieval session with Christina, which lasted several hours, her shamanic skills quickly revealed some of my core problems and gave me a peek into the evolution of my soul. For my session, we went to a small private room and lay side by side on blankets and pillows with our eyes shut. Christina asked of Spirit, "What does Diana need to heal?" Using her shamanic journeying skills, she entered the superconscious realm and reported back to me what she heard and saw about the times in my life when trauma had caused me to give up and shut down portions of my soul. As she told me what she saw, my intuition understood the symbolism. She was accurate.

Christina reported, "Lifetime after lifetime, steps along a path, there is a theme of love and also a theme of loss, this effort to learn about love. This lifetime you are bringing together the lessons of many lifetimes. You are at a phase of expansion in different expressions of love, the invisible world, nature, loved ones on the other side. You have come by this through experiences of great loss." She saw that in this life, death had taken the role of ally, of spirit helper, to invite me to live more fully and passionately and to develop the capacity for self-love. She said that in each of my lives there was one aspect that was not yet realized, and each lifetime was carrying me to the next step toward wholeness.

After explaining the purpose death had played in my life, she moved on to see a young version of me, a child out in nature, staying very close to a river. The child was like a little turtle that had lost its protective shell. "This aspect of you as a child carries a high level of sensitivity that is beyond the five senses. You are sensing more than is obvious to everyone else; you see five thousand bits and they see fifty bits. What you see is not validated by others, and you are not able to create your own natural sense of boundaries. You are learning behavior to fit into the system by saying only fifty bits are real."

I recognized that that was me in my childhood. In truth, I had quit listening to my inner guidance and deferred to others, ignoring the wisdom of my own heart. The soul of my inner child had shut down and given up trying to speak to me. I did not believe in myself. Christina talked to the child and invited her to return to me. She assured her that she would be safe and welcome now.

After our session ended, it was my job to go home and communicate with the part of me that had returned. Christina explained that when a soul part shuts down, we lose the gift associated with that soul part. In this integration work, we welcome back the parts of ourselves we neglected to heal in the past and ask, What gift do you bring?

During my early childhood I saw the beauty in the world; I was awed by its sparkle and shine. As I began conforming to the structure of civilization, my laughter, imagination, and ability to preserve memories through art was lost bit by bit. I remembered those days as I began my integration work. I apologized to the child, welcomed her return, and asked, What gift do you bring? Warm energy welled up in my heart, words and melody formed, and the child sang. Her song was a call to once again see the beauty, to play, and to use my imagination and my skills to capture memories.

Song of My Inner Child

I bring beauty, you love beauty,
I bring beauty, once again to your heart.
All around you, there is beauty,
take what you see and make a memory.
Don't walk the path without seeing the flowers.
Don't hurry by and miss all the messages.
Take your time just to feel, just to live and to be.
Let me breathe in you.

I am the child of your heart, I bring the laughter and play.
I am the one who gives you wings to fly away.
I bring the joy and the laughter, I bring the sparkle and shine.
Don't forget all the good times, don't forget the sublime.

After this reunion with my inner child, my joy increased tremendously. I sang the song over and over and delighted in the message. I began painting again. One morning I woke with an idea for a new painting sparkling in my mind. While in the dream state, I saw sunshine dancing on water, sand, and rocks in the river flowing by my lower yard. I began immediately, painted *Molalla River Rocks*, and hung the painting in the front entrance of my home. As the song encouraged me to do, I took what I saw and made a memory.

My life became richer and richer as I allowed the childlike wonder to expand. Jesus taught, become like children. Children explore and play, have no malice, and follow their heart. I learned to stop working and play when I wanted to play. I put on music and danced all by myself. When I sat alone and watched a sunset, I remembered what Jesus had once whispered in my heart, *I will hold your hand and watch the sunset with you.* I chose to be grateful. As the sun set, I would thank him and all the invisible spirits that constantly served humanity and me. I thanked the wind, the trees, the birds, the river for their contributions to my life.

I learned how to honor the inner nudges and follow my happy thoughts. I called it following my happy. In 2018, I followed my happy and went with a spiritually focused group led by Debra Stangl, founder of Sedona Soul

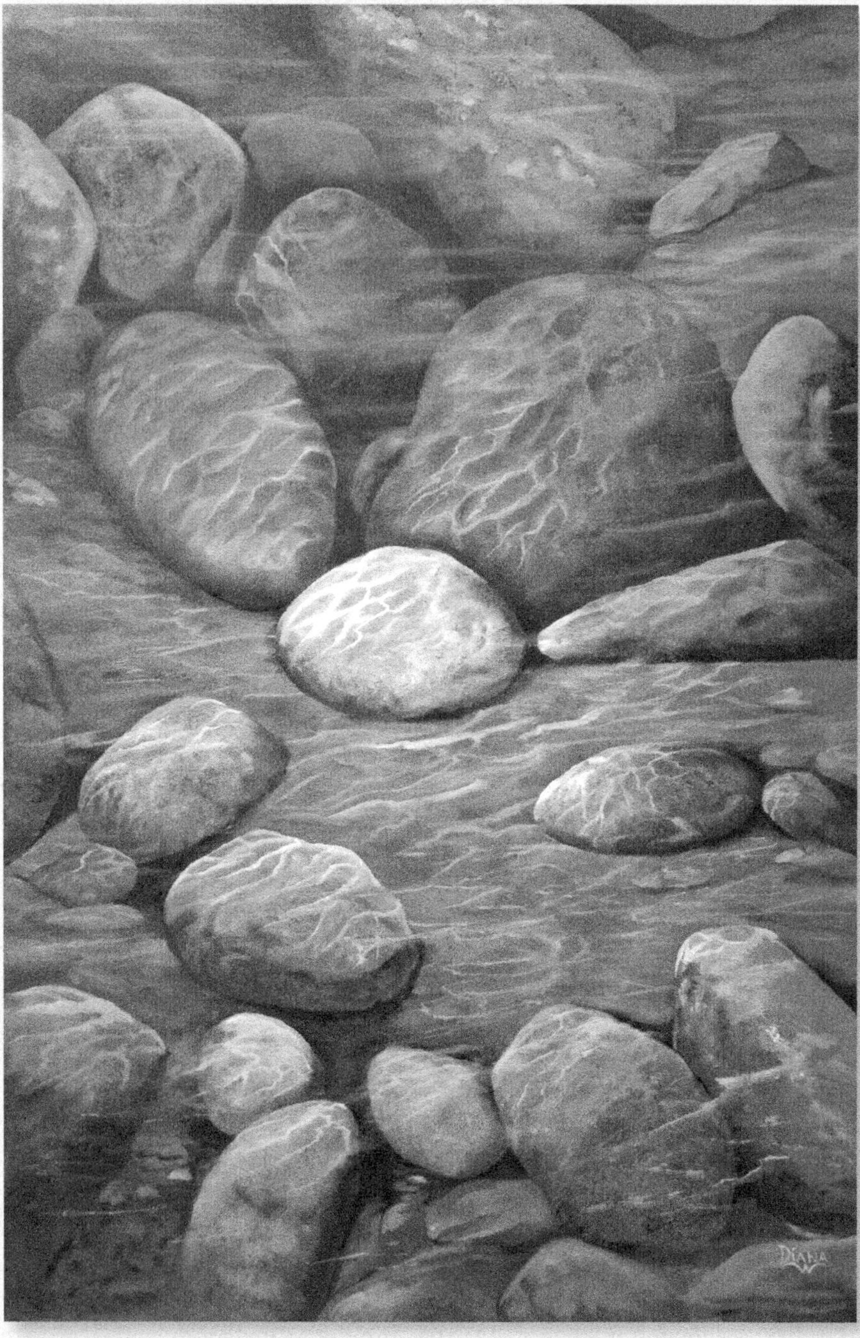
DIANA

Adventures, on a tour of Egypt. Debra's knowledge and experience made the tour a delight. She designed an itinerary that nurtured us spiritually and included all the must see sites of Egypt. It was an unforgettable experience where I danced, rode a camel, cruised the Nile, touched the Sphinx, and crawled on my hands and knees inside a pyramid. In September 2018, I returned to Sedona for a second soul adventure; this time, the adventure was solely for fun, a time to celebrate; it was a birthday gift to myself. Every year I looked for ways to enrich my life without and within. I *flowed with the energies that moved me* and went on adventures wherever my heart guided me.

※

Life became more delightful as I incorporated the wisdom of Spirit and others into my life. All of the lessons I had learned were combining and becoming light for my path. The messages over many months of learning—*flow with the energies that move you, nurture yourself, don't hurry by and miss all the messages, become as a child*—were guiding me in my daily choices. One day I woke with the desire to spend an entire day outside in relationship with the forest and the river. My acre of land on the river was the perfect playground. There were some areas of the river I could not access because brush blocked the way. I played explorer, cleared a new path, and uncovered logs and rocks near the river's edge. These provided a unique vantage point, beckoning me to sit, listen to the rippling river, and bask in the sunshine.

I removed my shoes and put my feet in the sparkling cool water. I talked to the trees, watched and listened to the birds. I stayed and played until the sun began to set. After walking the trail back to my house, I stood on my back deck overlooking the river. What is that? The water in the bay between the two rivers was boiling with activity. I pulled my cell phone from my jeans pocket and focused my video camera on the movement. I saw large brown bodies surfacing and submerging. One, two, three of them, moving like seals. What are they? My video camera stayed focused on the bubbling water, and one by one, they started moving upstream over the rocks. River otters, big ones!

I had never seen them before; what a delight! The sun dropped lower in the sky as they moved upriver. What was the spiritual significance of crossing paths with river otters? Native Americans honor the messages of animal sightings, and I had adopted this wisdom from them. Seeing otters play in the bay was a once-in-a-lifetime incident. I went inside to search the internet and was delighted to learn that crossing paths with otters symbolizes the inner child's release. I had let my inner child have her way for an entire day. These otters were messengers reflecting back to me. The universe was rejoicing with me because I had learned to play again.

I also had learned to pay attention to all the clues the universe brought my way. When I encountered Spirit through butterflies, herons, eagles, owls, and feathers, I honored the messages they conveyed.

One day in the summer of 2018, I was writing this book and reviewing Yana's words from my soul adventure the year before, "Your paintings are going to be transmissions." I felt Spirit moving and heard the voice within: *Listen to her, she speaks truth to you.* That week, I began a painting with no plan except to allow Spirit to flow. First came a figure eight, the infinity symbol; then a horse, a symbol of freedom and overcoming. It was pure joy letting inspiration flow as I added feathers, waterfalls, clouds, and bubbles. As I painted these symbols of truth, strength, honor, clarity, and higher thoughts, the painting became an expression of our uniqueness and infinite freedom to chose. I titled the painting *Infinity*.

THERE IS NO REVERSE GEAR

As I continued searching for ways to bring more joy into my life as a widow, I looked backward for memories of happy times. Remembering a midsize American Eskimo dog named Lady who had been dear to me, I decided to adopt another dog that looked like her. I visualized cuddling with her and taking walks together, just like I had with Lady. The happy day arrived when the breeder called and told me to come and pick out a puppy. I felt some uncertainty when I met the puppies, but I brushed it aside. I chose a bright-eyed, high-spirited little ball of pure white fluff and brought her home.

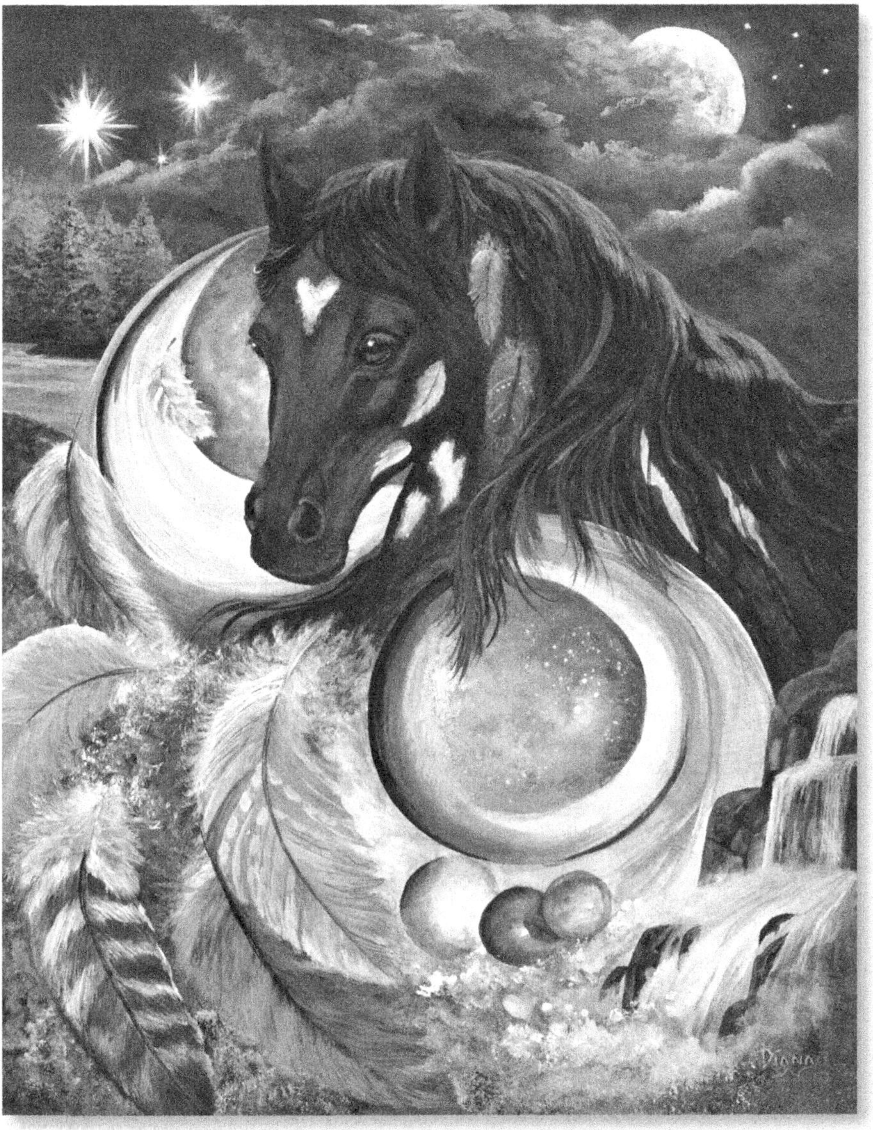
Diana

From the onset, I began to realize Crystal was nothing like Lady. She wanted constant action. There were moments of joy but many times of wondering if I had made a mistake. For many months I tried working with various dog trainers to calm her down and make the relationship work, but it just was not happening. Crystal was a dog who needed a different kind of lifestyle from what I could provide. She needed an owner who could satisfy her need for activity.

My heart told me to find her a new home. I grieved inwardly, knowing that both of us would experience pain, and realized I was dead center in the middle of another lesson in growth. I recognized that I was using a Band-Aid to cover a wound. The wound was loneliness, and Crystal was the Band-Aid. I had reached into yesterday's memories to try to find a solution for today's problem. The way of Spirit is forward, not backward. From this experience, I learned you don't go back. You can't fix the present moment by reproducing the past.

I faced the reality that Crystal needed a family with children who could romp and play with her every minute. With the help of the breeder, I found the perfect home for my pedigree, hyper, beautiful little dog. I prepared a small manual that contained all the words Crystal understood and activities she enjoyed, and made a five-minute video about her routine that her new family could watch so they could help her transition. I packed Crystal's belongings, and the family and I met halfway between their home in Idaho and mine in Oregon.

The moment of transferring Crystal to their car was painful for me. I saw her questioning eyes peering out through her crate. After saying goodbye, I headed home, stopping briefly at Baskin-Robbins to comfort myself with a chocolate ice cream cone. The new family soon reported back to me that the children took her out for so many walks that she would fall sound asleep after she came back home. Crystal was the darling of their local park, and all the children loved to run and play with her. It was a massive relief to me that Crystal was happy and had what she needed. Still, back home without her, I cried, knowing I would not see her pretty face come to me when I called her name.

It was another discovery for me: doing the right thing sometimes hurts. In life, there is no reverse gear, but it is safe to follow the inner guidance forward. There are many new joys to be found.

To everything, there is a season. After three years of renovating the River House, I noticed my enthusiasm waning. I was baffled but continued to find things on the acre of land or in the home that I could improve. My life was being consumed by manual labor, and once again I thought about moving. I passed several months working and wondering why the energetic flow was gone.

I decided to spend an entire day focusing on getting a response from Spirit. My prayer on Sunday, May 24, 2020, was: "I want to move forward and discover more of this life, but there is no place I know of that has the beauty of nature so near to home as the River House has. I love the river. I need the wisdom and guidance only you can provide. When *you* guide, I know what to do, and I have comfort."

The voice within responded:

> *Stay where you are. This hunger for change is not about moving physically, it is about moving spiritually. It is your quest for truth; it is the process of discovery. Your home is now what you wanted it to be. You can be settled and at rest to grow, unfold your wings, and fly to the places you are led to. Don't move out of the home, just move out of the rut of repairing it. Enjoy it, enjoy your life, and expand your borders. Stay and continue to flourish.*

Oh my, I had gotten into a rut again! I realized I needed to make a change. The renovation had provided experiences and challenges. It had induced paradigm shifts and built more skills and virtues into my character. The qualities of compassion, resilience, strength, patience, perseverance, balance, joy, acceptance, trust, and self-nurture had grown within me. But now I was ready to move on to the next phase of my life, further unleashing my creativity. As my River House was now a beautiful home, my haven, I decided to focus on increasing my skills as a fine artist and learning the writer's craft.

I was excited to see where the evolution of my artistic talent would lead me. Over the years, I had heard the whisper of Spirit: *You need to paint.* I was a bit embarrassed at not taking action sooner. I now scheduled my days around painting, writing, and enjoying the river in my backyard. Developing illustrations and working on my manuscript was a good blend.

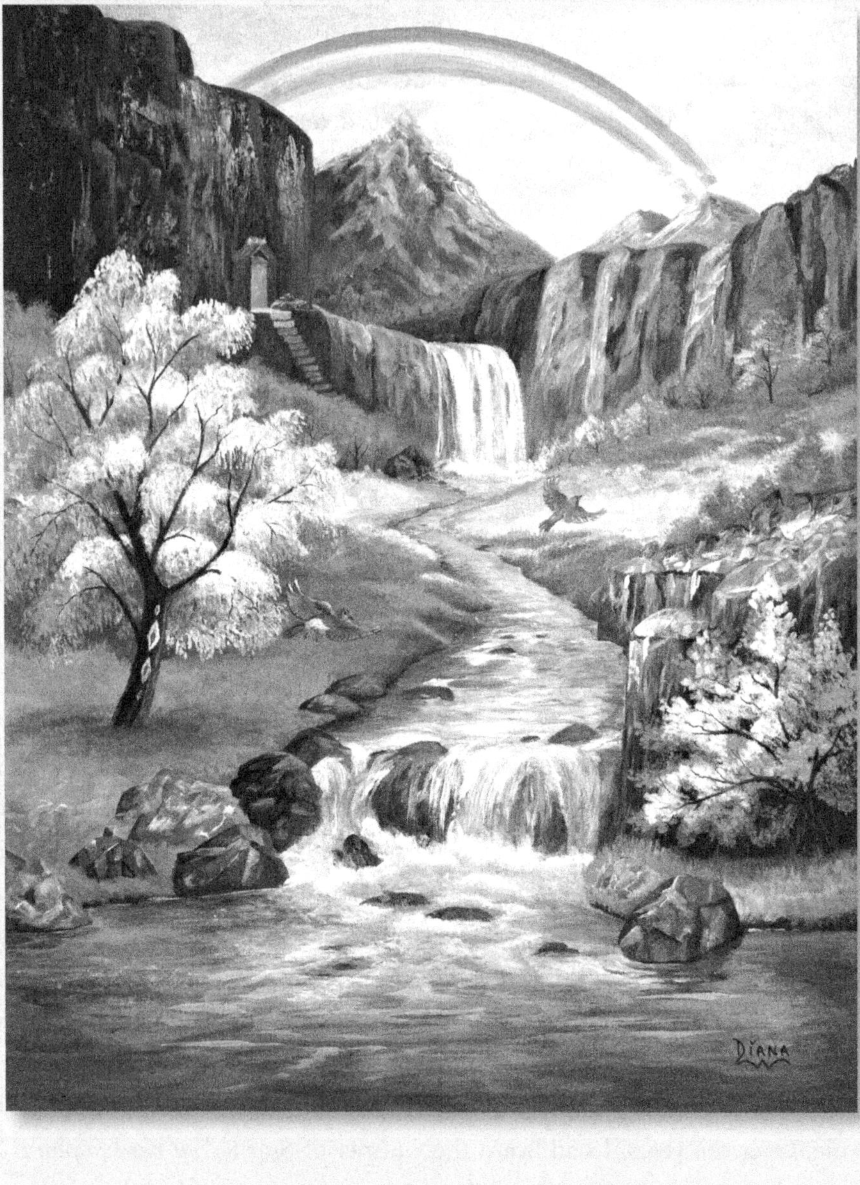
DIANA

Within me was a desire to paint intuitively and allow imagination free rein. Formerly I had focused mainly on realistic scenes and emphasizing the beauty of wildlife and nature. One night, I had a dream where I saw a valley adorned with rainbow colors; it became my inspiration. I began painting without a carefully crafted design and allowed myself the freedom to paint with the joy of an unrestrained child. Rainbow Valley's rocks became crystals, and the mountainside featured a staircase leading to an entryway. I imagined crossing the valley, walking up the stairs, going through the doorway, and entering the mountain. Wise teachers would greet me and share their knowledge with me within that mountain. Birds filled the sky; crystals adorned the stream. It was pure joy as I played and created a perfect imaginary place.

Painting and writing were my new companions, and I was in the flow, enjoying the creative process. I prayed, asking what I should share in my book to benefit others. At unexpected times fully formed sentences would flood into my mind and perfectly communicate what I struggled to write. Those downloads were glorious moments; I quickly captured the precious words for use in my manuscript. My story became another platform Spirit used to help me grow, evolve, and voice my truth.

Music was another outlet. I had placed an electronic piano keyboard in front of the large picture window overlooking the river. One day I was playing a simple melody and singing a song that had come to me spontaneously from my heart as I watched the river steadily moving downstream.

Flow River Flow

Flow river flow on your way to the sea,
Follow the path leading to your destiny.
Return to me in the falling rain,
Come again in snowflakes and the dew.
Be mist upon the mountaintop,
Fog across the sea,
Put sparkle in a baby's eyes,
Be all you're meant to be.
Flow river flow on your way to the sea,
Follow your path and come again to me.

I suddenly realized that all along, I had been singing a song of release to Mark. The river always flows continuously, effortlessly, beautifully performing its task. No one can stop it. The river does not flow backward; it continues; it changes, transformed in multiple ways: as fog, ice, falling rain, snow, or dew. My song to the river was one of acceptance, accepting that change in this life is inevitable. It was a song of release, letting go of that which was gone and past. It was also a song of recognition that we are infinite, eternal. There is no end, only change.

We don't just pass; we continue; we transition. I had attained upward growth. I had come to realize that change is a good thing, a reality that needs to be embraced rather than feared. We never die, and death does not separate us. The presence of our loved ones is always available to us even after death. I now knew this from experience; it was not just a belief. Mark was simply in a different dimension of reality. I sang the words knowing that Mark and I would meet again in a different realm than we had known as husband and wife.

15

In Search of Truth

As I was renovating my River House, I was also simultaneously crossing a bridge, searching for answers. In the early morning or late evening, I would read books, pray, and meditate. Many questions about the truth of my long-held beliefs were bubbling up to the surface of my awareness. I needed to find answers to calm the tides of my soul. My beliefs had been a significant anchor in my life but had proved insufficient during my most recent trauma. Being introduced to new perspectives was what had restored my hope. Joy and vitality were flowing in my spirit, and these refreshing emotions came as a direct result of a new mindset. Who was right? I wanted to be sure I was re-anchoring my life on solid ground. I had work to do.

One of the healers I consulted in Sedona used the term *fear-based doctrines*. I had never thought of my beliefs as fear-based and was surprised by the implication. At age sixteen, in an all-or-nothing gulp, I had followed the crowd. I had ignored my intuition and given my power over to religious leaders, starting a lifelong tendency. When I asked Jesus into my life, I accepted everything leaders in my church taught me. I accepted the way others interpreted portions of the Bible.

I recalled the words Spirit spoke to me when I was in Sedona: *You are entering a new chapter called evolution.* I was taking a major leap forward, away from being guided by others, trusting that Spirit could guide me for the rest of my days. I had been blessed and validated by Spirit when I followed my heart and went to Sedona. Spirit had met me and given me a taste of having my own experience, so now I saw no need to settle for less. My worldview had expanded. I felt like I had lived a great deal of my life with my head buried in the sand of other people's beliefs, ideas, and decisions. Now I wanted to find my own truth.

I thought about the healers in Sedona who had left fear-based religions. Their enthusiasm and excitement about their relationship with Jesus/Jeshua was undeniable. I reflected on their terminology; they spoke of Light or Christ consciousness. They were self-guided by the light within, not community guided or under a pastor's authority. The independence these people had was new to me. They were the first people I had met who spoke of a relationship with Jesus in the absence of fear-based doctrines. I did not know people could choose Jesus and not believe all the doctrines associated with him.

I could see that not all followers of the Light/Christ believed the same things. These people were as genuine as any I had ever met; their healing methods were effective. They were serving Spirit without the weight of fear that I carried. Their perspectives and spiritual gifts, coupled with the work of Spirit, had changed my entire outlook on life, loss, and pain. My transformation had taken only four days.

Now my goal was to examine doctrines that I thought were infallible and collect guidance that would help me steer by my own stars. I wanted to live a purposeful life in harmony with the divinity I saw in the universe. No longer was I going to believe doctrines simply because many others accepted them. I wanted only truth as the foundation of my life. Researching historical sacred text was where I would start.

※

I began the daunting task of searching through the tangled web of historical philosophies, beliefs, religions, and doctrines. I searched relentlessly for months, as one seeking gold. I traced the evolution of the Bible and created a four-page timeline of related events. I dug to find the origins of specific fear-based doctrines and the concept of reincarnation. I studied the conflicting doctrines and sometimes became bewildered. Books, books, books, everyone has a different viewpoint! At last, I did find the answers and the relief I sought.

I identified three main doctrines focused on shame, guilt, and judgment. All three doctrines have faulty foundations. Mistranslation was one factor, and lack of scriptural basis was another. Jesus never taught these three doctrines, and the early church did not believe them. All three are theories originating in the minds of men that were passed down over time and blindly accepted in Western Christianity. Finally, though, many Christians and scholars are writing books and providing documented evidence that these three doctrines are leading us in the wrong direction.

I went through a series of emotions as I found the trail of truth. First I was shocked that I had believed theories rather than God's truth. I realized I had accepted fear-based doctrines because I was conditioned to believe and respect authority. I thought all doctrines originated from the highest divine authority, so I blindly accepted even doctrines I thought were deplorable. Now I know those deplorable doctrines originated in the minds of men.

Then I started to feel afraid because the doctrines are still mainstream. I thought, What am I going to do with this information? My Christian friends will think I am crazy! Then I realized that the best response to these theories is right before our eyes. The fear-based doctrines can easily be replaced by the good news found in scripture.

※

The first fear-based doctrine is original sin, the idea that children are born unclean and are guilty before God. The doctrine probably began to form among church fathers two or three centuries after Christ died but was first named in writing and promoted by Augustine of Hippo (354–430 AD), who based his belief on the story of Adam and Eve in Genesis. Augustine was not a Greek scholar, and his theory came from his own mistranslation of scripture and by cobbling various passages together. The doctrine of original sin effectively degrades people and brings them down to their knees in guilt.

The good news is that Jesus did not teach that children are born unclean or sinful. He pointed to children as models for us to learn from. He commended the children with these words: "See that you do not despise one of these little ones. For I tell you that their angels in heaven always see the face of my Father in heaven" (Matthew 18:10). He said the kingdom of God is within and if we are like children we can enter it. "He called a little child to him, and placed the child among them. And he said: 'Truly I tell you, unless you change and become like little children, you will never enter the kingdom of heaven'" (Matthew 18:2).

I was pleased to be able to replace the theory with real scripture that was good news. We are not born as sinners, but we are born into a world that can lure us into things that don't benefit us. Jesus came to give us the power to overcome the things in this world that take us down and put us into bondage.

※

The second fear-based doctrine is that Jesus had to die to pay for our sins. My research uncovered that nothing in the Bible says this. In truth, Anselm, archbishop of Canterbury, formulated this doctrine in the eleventh century. In an interview in *US Catholic* in November 2018 entitled "No One Had to Die for Our Sins," theologian Elizabeth Johnson explains that Anselm got the idea from the feudal society he lived in. With no police force or armies, the word of a lord was law. If you broke a law, you had to pay back to the lord to restore order. Anselm took that political arrangement as the way the universe works. God is the lord of this world and we have to pay back for sinning and breaking God's law. The last part of his theory was, Jesus was sinless so did not deserve to die, but humans have sinned so deserve to die. Jesus died to pay back something that God was owed that humans couldn't pay back.

Finding out that this doctrine was man-made really upset me at first, because I thought I would be disrespecting Jesus if I did not believe it. Then the light of understanding came. It is semantics. His death was a victory for us, not a payment for our sins, which is a man-invented phrase and theory. Anselm's theory leaves out the fact that God forgives sin and has never asked for payment for sin. "For I will be merciful toward their iniquities, and I will remember their sins no more" (Hebrews 8:12); "I am he who blots out your transgressions for my own sake, and I will not remember your sins" (Isaiah 43:25); "As far as the east is from the west, so far does he remove our transgressions from us" (Psalm 103:12).

Did Jesus suffer in order to help us? A resounding yes to that! "He was wounded for our transgressions, he was bruised for our iniquities: the chastisement of our peace was upon him; and with his stripes we are healed" (Isaiah 53:5). It is clear that we gained because he gave his life to help us, but his life was not a required payment for our sins; he was not appeasing an angry God. The idea that God is so cruel that he would sacrifice his own son to appease his anger is totally contrary to the message of Jesus and the reality of God's own words of love for humanity. "I have loved you with an everlasting love; I have drawn you with unfailing kindness" (Jeremiah 31:3); "I have engraved you on the palms of my hands" (Isaiah 49:16).

Jesus said, "I came that they may have life, and may have it abundantly" (John 10:10). Writings by his disciple John say he came to give us power: "But as many as received him, to them gave he power to become the sons of God, even to them that believe on his name" (John 1:12). His good news was that the kingdom of God is in us and we are in it. Jesus said, "You won't be able to say, 'Here it is!' or 'It's over there!' For the Kingdom of God is already among you" (Luke 17:21). His good news is that he gave us authority over anything that would harm us: "I have given you authority to trample on snakes and scorpions and to overcome all the power of the enemy; nothing will harm you" (Luke 10:19).

�֎

The third fear-based doctrine is that the wicked, including all those who aren't Christian (and thus unbaptized babies), are destined for hell, a place of eternal torment, after death. It seems that Augustine of Hippo is once again the responsible party here, cementing this concept in the Western churches. His two theories, of original sin and of eternal damnation, support each other, suggesting that all will suffer endless torment if they don't convert to his theology.

The good news I found is that the early church did not believe in eternal torment. Their texts reveal that Jesus taught reincarnation and universal salvation. References to reincarnation, and early church sacred texts supporting it, were removed or left out of the Bible. Pastor Keith Giles, in his book *Jesus Undefeated: Condemning the False Doctrine of Eternal Torment,* does a marvelous job of revealing the mistranslations that suggest Jesus taught hell. "People who believe in hell create it for themselves and others" was the realization of one pastor, Carlton Pearson, who lost his congregation when he questioned the existence of hell.

✺

There is a doctrine stating the Bible is the "infallible word of God." I believed that teaching, and it produced fear in me and controlled my actions for five decades. To find the source of this doctrine, I traced the three-thousand-year history of the Bible. I created a timeline, starting with the Torah, which dates to 1400 BC and gave us the first five books of the Bible. I noted the Council of Nicea in 325 AD convened by the Roman emperor Constantine, where original sin was first invented; virgin birth was established as a fact…without any evidence; the Gospel of Thomas was eliminated because it quoted Jesus as saying there is a divine spark in each person; the Gospel of Mark was altered to include the resurrection story; and sacred text that spoke of the divine feminine was altered or omitted. This was the time when Romans attempted to destroy any gospels that did not conform to their ideas.

I charted how Augustine of Hippo cemented the doctrines of hell and original sin, how reincarnation was declared as heresy at the Second Council of Constantinople in 553 AD, and how the doctrine of original sin was formalized as part of Roman Catholic doctrine at the Council of Trent in 1546. I noted that the Gnostic texts, many of them written by contemporaries and disciples of Jesus, were discovered in Nag Hammadi, Egypt, in 1945, and that the Dead Sea Scrolls, more than eight hundred documents that deepen our understanding of the Bible and shed light on the histories of Judaism and Christianity, were discovered over a period of years by Bedouin shepherds and archaeologists in the mid-twentieth century.

In the process of creating my timeline, I found that not every word in the Bible is God-breathed scripture. I learned that culture, politics, bias, mistranslations, and human reasoning have all affected the contents of the Bible and the doctrines that followed. There are forty-one thousand different Bible-based denominations, each with its own interpretations of the text. Some have different Bibles, varying from sixty-six to seventy-three books. The Bible does include scripture, defined as the sacred writings of religion, but scripture makes up only part of the Bible. The Bible also contains contradictions, history, genealogies, letters, and stories handed down for centuries.

In a study about translation errors, I came across two different translations of 2 Timothy 3:16.

> Incorrect: "All scripture is given by inspiration of God."
>
> Correct: "All God-breathed scripture is profitable for doctrine."

I saw how easily this mistranslation could have evolved into making the Bible equal to God's word.

I have seen how scriptures can influence people to accomplish wonderful and good things. Many times a Bible verse has comforted, inspired, or guided me. In those moments, the text seems to come alive with the love, wisdom, and compassionate presence of Spirit. I know firsthand that there are Spirit-inspired scriptures in the Bible because they speak to me and lift me. I have also seen people justify controlling, harming, and judging others based on interpretations of scripture. History is strewn with so-called holy wars, the bloody fruit of misguided religious beliefs. The mistakes I have made in my life have come by ignoring my inner warning light and submitting to other people's interpretation of scripture.

After my research, I looked at the Bible I had treasured and wondered which parts were Spirit speaking and which were tainted by errors of human reasoning. I see no need to throw out the good with the bad. The answer to which verses are Spirit-breathed is within me. The light within us responds to truth; it is our soul connection to our Source. That light is my guide; my internal compass feels joy when the truth is present. Our emotions respond to words of truth; we experience encouragement, inspiration, wisdom, and happiness.

We fuel our inner light every time we focus on our eternal relationship with Spirit. When we acknowledge the higher power, the All That Is, when we ask for guidance, when we express gratitude, when we love each other, the light grows brighter. Awareness of and following the guidance of our inner light is the fastest route to truth, peace, and purpose. The light is what responded in me when I was in Sedona. Loving words fueled my inner light and removed self-condemnation and religious bondage. Spirit-breathed words helped me, fear and doubt fled, and joy surfaced.

Words that are Spirit-breathed fill the heart with a knowing that you are loved, supported, and guided. Spirit speaks throughout creation, through every form, to those who will listen. In short, words that judge, create fear, bring you down, depress, enslave, and make you feel less than loved are not Spirit-breathed. All are loved. What we do to one, we do to all, including ourselves, as we are One. These three words are Spirit-breathed: "Love one another."

※

There is a void, the mystery beyond life on earth. We have an unquenchable curiosity about what lies beyond the veil. We want to know what happens after physical death. In the early phase of my life, I put a Band-Aid on that void by accepting the church's ideas of heaven and hell. The Band-Aid was never totally comfortable, and it began to come loose when Mark said, "Diana, there is no hell." That was the first time in my life I had heard that news; I wanted it to be so, as it *felt* good. Then healers in Sedona spoke of reincarnation, universal redemption, and the continual processes of soul growth. The relief and joy I felt when their words entered my heart motivated me to find my truth. I had options!

Reincarnation is a concept believed by millions throughout history and around the world today. My research showed me that in 800 BC, the concept of reincarnation was recorded in the Upanishads, philosophical and religious texts composed in Sanskrit. The idea was also entertained by some ancient Greek philosophers. In the fourth to fifth century BC, Plato held that the soul is immortal and participates in frequent incarnations. Reincarnation is in the Gnostic gospels of the first century AD. One of these, the Gospel of Philip, reveals, "Light and darkness, life and death, and right and left are siblings of one another, and inseparable. For this reason the good are not good, the bad are not bad, life is not life, death is not death. For this reason each one will dissolve into its earliest origin, but what is superior to the world cannot be dissolved, for it is eternal" (as translated by Marvin Meyer in the Gnostic Society Library, www.gnosis.org).

A couple of centuries after the birth of Christ, the prolific Christian scholar Origen of Alexandria explained reincarnation in his concept of "the restoration of all things." But the teaching of Jesus promising the restoration of all God's children was removed from Christianity in 553 AD at the Second Council of Constantinople, where the writings of Origen and others were declared anathema. Romans left the Gnostic texts out of the Bible because they reveal that the early Christians accepted reincarnation, redemption for all, and growth of the eternal soul as a fact. To allow the belief in reincarnation would ruin all the man-made doctrine the church fathers had created over the years and prove that the institution of the Church isn't the only option to bring eternal life to people.

My view of this world and all the worlds within worlds beyond our present view has changed. For me, insight into reincarnation and universal salvation is not another Band-Aid covering the mysterious void beyond earthly life. It removes the need for a Band-Aid and gives me peace.

The case studies in Michael Newton's books *Journey of Souls* and *Destiny of Souls* document people's memories of life between lives. They tell of the ongoing process of life, life review, another life, life review, another life, and so on. As I read the case studies, I marveled, and scriptures softly floated through my memory. "He will wipe every tear from their eyes, and there will be no more death or sorrow or crying or pain. All these things are gone forever" (Revelation 21:4). The fairness of the process described in the case studies answers every question I have ever had about life.

After reading about reincarnation, I put the pieces together into a new understanding. Of my own free will, I incarnated to earth. I agreed to incarnate into this life and its experiences because my growth would be of service to all. Those in my life have been with me eternally, playing different roles. Some are soulmates; we are all helping each other grow. Life circumstances are the kettle that removes the dross and produces the gold. During the entire journey on earth and elsewhere, we are never alone, never without support. We are eternal. The light within each of us is our connection to All That Is. It is our receiver, our guide. We are all one with Spirit. This new understanding takes away the sting of death and loss; it takes away the feeling of separation from loved ones.

My own life verifies what I have learned about reincarnation. When I look back, I see that all my losses have eventually led to gains. Four times in my life, I have faced that challenge, and finally I have the understanding that has allowed me to let go. I no longer look at a loss with regret; I see it as the flow of life, the necessity of change to achieve a greater purpose. Being crushed has led to compassion, acceptance of others, and a new worldview. I think of the words my husband Tom once said: "Our misery is our ministry." I think of Jesus during his crucifixion. He demonstrated compassion and knowledge by saying, "Forgive them, for they know not what they do" (Luke 23:34).

At one point, as I thought about the anger and pain I felt when Mark died, and as I reflected on reincarnation, a point of understanding flooded my brain. I shouted out loud, "Mark!…you mean to tell me that we planned this?!" I was changed from that moment on. I saw that Mark was a soulmate helping me evolve and grow. He drew me with love. His views, his method, and finally, his early death shook my world and catapulted me out of my rut. Without that loss, I would have stayed in my little tiny drip of light and never gone to Sedona. My need for answers as a result of that loss led me to find a stream of light flowing out from the souls of history and the souls shining their lights in our world today.

My new understanding of reincarnation has done several things for me.

I now feel at liberty to speak to my loved ones in the spirit realm. I know they are right here, even though I don't see them. I have found extra significance in words Jesus spoke to humanity: "I am in you," "I am with you always," "I will never leave you or forsake you." When I read the joyful accounts of worlds within worlds that provide every soul with every joy and opportunity one could desire, they reminded me of Jesus' words, "There is more than enough room in my Father's home. If this were not so, would I have told you that I am going to prepare a place for you?" (John 14:2). Seeing the infinity of life and the onward growth of each soul, I feel grateful for the time I have had with others. I know there are infinitely more times ahead to interact with them.

I am able to honor the sacred path of others. I feel some shame in knowing that at one time, I gave no merit to religious and spiritual paths that differed from my own. Through the lens of reincarnation, I now see that each path is perfect for the one who walks thereon. Each experience of life gives another vantage point, an opportunity to grow and gain understanding, enabling that soul to accept and love others. Each person is unique and has a valuable part to play in their chosen sphere. Each has the right to learn, unfold, and grow as their inner light directs them.

I no longer compartmentalize people: high/low, believer/unbeliever, saved/lost, friend/foe, right/wrong, Democrat/Republican, king/pauper, achiever/failure, rich/poor. It is not the way of Spirit to place all people into one mold or deny them the joy of free choice. Spirit is more than able to reach any heart. To believe that we need to convert others to our way of thinking resembles arrogance and lack of faith in Spirit. The good news we are to share is not about making all people conform to our thinking. Let your light shine with good works, love one another, and do not judge one another: these are basic to the message of Jesus.

I have learned that all have light, guidance leading them on a path for their well-being. Each person's life experience is tailored to help them become the best version of themselves. The ultimate pinnacle of each soul is to become so filled with the light that nothing remains but the light. Sometimes we can shine our light and help others kindle their flame. Another Gnostic text, the

Gospel of Thomas, quotes Jesus, "Light exists within a person of light, and they light up the whole world. If they don't shine, there's darkness" (as translated by Mark M. Mattison on Gospels.net).

I have learned to look for the gift in life experiences. I can see the blessings that have come from my challenges and obstacles. The many changes in my beliefs are a colossal gift. My perspective on life trials has changed; my viewpoint on others has changed. I have gained a new reason for living, to climb higher toward the goal of being pure light. Insights into the brilliant and highly sophisticated processes of reincarnation have elevated my confidence in the Spirit guiding our universe. Spirit is far more resourceful than humanity and does not need to resort to human methods of fear, guilt, shame, torment. Spirit enables through love.

❦

During the time when I was researching ancient and new sources of wisdom and knowledge, all the sources I studied led me right back to my own heart.

I learned that science has confirmed what wisdom has long affirmed. It is our heart, not our mind, that is the master orchestrator in our life. Each person has a built-in capacity to be receptive to Spirit's wisdom. The healers in Sedona advised me, do things that bring you joy, do what inspires you, and you will heal. I had to start at ground zero, shut out the fear of other people's opinions, and focus on my own heart and inner guidance. After that, it became easy to recognize which path I am to take. I just have to listen to my heart and follow the wisdom it offers. I learned that joy is the green light, the go-ahead signal from the heart. If I feel hesitancy or fear in my heart, it is a no-go, a red light.

I gained much of this understanding by honoring others and listening to what they had learned. From Eastern and Western texts, ancient and new, I heard many terms used to describe the laws that affect all of humanity. I read about laws of vibration, attraction, divine oneness, and cause and effect, to name only a few. I learned we are all connected and affected by the same laws. Whether we call it the kingdom within, the divine spark, or the light within, we are all part of this one cosmos. I saw that religious doctrines that divide and separate humanity into groups are products of limited human thinking.

Some of my greatest joys came after learning the ancient knowledge of Native Americans, Indigenous tribes, and Eastern wisdom. When I understood that Spirit is in all the cosmos, not just in humans, I was overjoyed! I embraced a new worldview where all, including trees, animals, wind, air, fire, water, rocks, and stars, are conscious. I have new friends; we are energetically connected, part of the one Spirit, and can communicate with each other. I went outside and apologized to creation for being so arrogant and not realizing it was conscious. I spoke to the beautiful evergreen trees in my yard and the river flowing by my property. The rocks, flowers, animals, birds, and stars have become my companions. When I watch and listen for Spirit speaking through the elements of nature, I am blessed over and over with beneficial messages.

I remembered many scriptures in the Bible that confirm that the earth and creatures have voice. "Speak to the earth, and it will teach you; and the fish of the sea will explain to you" (Job 12:8). Communication is done telepathically and accomplished when the mind is quiet and the breath is slowed down. As I studied, I learned that this ability is within all humans. The Seneca Indians would meditate on a hillside and listen to the mysteries rocks would speak of. The rocks would reveal the history of that area.

I read that all of the cosmos was created to love and support each other. The elements rejoice in our well-being. When I walk a forest path or feel the foam of an ocean wave come forward and touch my toes, I can greet all of nature as my friend. "The mountains and the hills shall break forth before you into singing, and all the trees of the field shall clap their hands" (Isaiah 55:12).

I now see our mother earth as our nourisher, teacher, friend, messenger; as one to be protected, nurtured, honored, and loved in return. "Hurt not the earth, neither the sea, nor the trees" (Revelation 7:3). Mother earth is our example, teaching us to live our lives in service, loving all, and contributing to the well-being of all. All that is on this earth, the galaxies, the spirit realm, is connected, a fact now verified by science. This wisdom has always been known and handed down for generations.

This awareness helped lift the loneliness from my life. The world is no longer an empty place; the loves of my life have not left me behind. They exist in a parallel universe, vibrationally not visible but totally accessible by telepathy. I am no longer alone, waiting for my departure to heaven. I matter. Spirit has reached into my life and given me a jump start.

※

If I had never ventured beyond the pages of the Bible, I would never have discovered the knowledge I needed to heal my grief. After realizing that the Bible is limited and does not have all the wisdom of the world, I searched through book after book looking for the truth. These writings expanded my horizons past what I ever could have imagined, but finally, I had three dreams that encouraged me to stop the search.

In the first dream, I see myself sitting up in my bed, my legs covered by blankets, a pillow across my lap, with piles of books on both sides of me. I place my hands on my face, lean forward at the waist, and bury my face in the pillow across my lap. I am weary from searching. I have not found one written source that has answered all my questions. In my dream, I say, "Father, I just want to know the truth." I hear the voice within reply, *It is day by day, instant by instant, Diana. There is no book. It is within you.* That was the end of the dream and the end of my search for *all* knowledge in books.

In another dream, I see Arizona desert and a black pavement highway ahead. A hill rises in front of my car and as I drive up the hill, I can't see beyond the crest. When I reach the top, the black pavement ends and before me is rough gravel road and then desert with no visible road. Voice within: *Don't fear the desert with no evidence of a road going anywhere. The plan is in place, the road is obscured only from your vision. Everything is under control. Everything is as it should be. Continue on and trust.* I now understand that we are given the knowledge we need, when we need it. There is no shame in not having answers to all the questions. Yogis consider it wisdom to say, "I don't know." This life for each of us has a purpose, and we need only the knowledge that applies to our current purpose on earth.

In a third dream about my quest for healing, the solution that kept coming to me was that I need to relax and enjoy life without constant concern for producing results. I need to nurture myself and let my Source and the universe do what they do best. I need only stay in alignment and live a balanced life. The universe will produce the results and arrange the best of circumstances. The voice within confirmed: *Alignment with Source, with Father and Mother Divine, with the laws of the universe results in the most profound place of peace. It also yields the highest productivity for the good of all. Striving to move forward is not necessary. All that is required is to daily pay attention to the details directly in front of you. Let joy and desire propel your actions.*

EPILOGUE

All One in Love

One day while working on the River House in early 2019, I was mentally assembling my thoughts about the book I would write. I experienced a download of Spirit energy and recorded these words in my journal:

> *This book will have a focus; that focus is that my children should not live in fear of me. I do not confine myself to man's religions.*

Of course! I could see that "fear not" was the lesson I had learned and the core message of my story. In my research, I discovered that the Hebrew words translated in the Bible as "fear," *yara*, *yirah*, or *yarah*, actually refer to "a flowing in your gut" that feels like "reverence, respect, awe" (according to *The Living Words* by Jeff A. Benner). So the Bible translation "fear the Lord" could just as easily be understood as "be in awe." "Be in awe" of this amazing Wisdom that cares about us! There is no need to fear.

As I looked back over what I had learned from history during my search for truth, I saw people trying to control others and to convert them to their beliefs. Withholding knowledge is a control method; in the fourth century, sacred texts were burned in an effort to control thinking. In my life, church leaders told me not to read books that did not conform to the Bible. Criticism is another method of control, as is adopting an attitude of superiority—looking down on others, labeling them, categorizing them, shunning them. People resort to attempts to control because of their own insecurities. To feel secure, they need to be surrounded by like-minded people who support their views. Fear drives them. They cannot stand alone.

I see my community of church friends as those who are as innocent as I was; we all thought we were hearing and defending truth. We thought we were honoring God by adhering to the fear-based doctrines of Anselm and Augustine. Not so! There is so much *really* good news that we don't need to burden ourselves and others with messages of fear and guilt. All of us who have experienced the Christ within know what that relationship is all about: an empowered life, a friend who is always with us, wisdom encapsulated into our inner being. A voice within that speaks and guides us.

There is a saying within some churches: Are you a believer? I would now respond, "Oh yes! I am a believer, and daily, I discover there is a whole lot more I believe in and a whole lot less to fear."

※

As I searched for the source of ultimate truth throughout the sacred writings of many spiritual disciplines, the best part for me was discovering where we agreed. It reminded me of Mark and myself. We thought we were so different, but our love for each other caused us to respect the other's viewpoint. He said it so well: "We are not so different, you and I."

Comparing the teachings of spiritual leaders side by side, I found agreement in many areas, starting with the Golden Rule.

> Buddhism: Treat not others in ways that you yourself would find harmful.
>
> Christianity: Do unto others as you would have them do unto you.
>
> Hinduism: Do not do to others what would cause pain if done to you.
>
> Islam: Not one of you truly believes until you wish for others what you wish for yourself.
>
> Judaism: What is hateful to you, do not do to your neighbor.

Sikhism: I am a stranger to no one; and no one is a stranger to me. Indeed, I am a friend to all.

Taoism: Regard your neighbor's gain as your own gain and your neighbor's losses as your own.

One spiritual leader who sought the essential unity in all religions was Swami Sri Yukteswar, a saint and a yogi renowned for his wisdom and discernment. His goal in a book he wrote in 1894 titled *The Holy Science* was to reveal where Eastern and Western sacred texts agree on fundamental truths. He documented his findings using a format of parallel passages, showing the Sanskrit of the East and the Holy Bible of the West side by side. As I was reading his book, I soon saw that both the Eastern and Western sacred texts respect the virtues and espouse principles defining how to live a life of integrity.

Eastern sacred text: There are eight bondages, snares, or meannesses of the human heart. Those eight are hatred, shame, fear, grief, condemnation, race prejudice, pride of pedigree, and a narrow sense of respectability. Those who act on these meannesses are far out of alignment with the Divine. Through the removal of these eight obstacles, magnanimity of the heart comes in.

Western sacred text: "Love is patient and kind. It does not envy or boast; it is not proud. It does not dishonor others; it is not self-seeking, it is not easily angered, it keeps no record of wrongs. Love does not delight in evil but rejoices with the truth. It always protects, always trusts, always hopes, always perseveres" (1 Corinthians 13:4-7).

While I was reading the Upanishads, it became apparent to me that the author of the text had experienced a spiritual awakening. The text speaks of finding the "Ancient One" in the innermost recess, hidden in "the cave of the heart." Here is the verse, written thousands of years ago: "The wise, who by means of the highest meditation on the Self knows the Ancient One, difficult to perceive, seated in the innermost recess, hidden in the cave of the heart, dwelling in the depth of inner being, (he who knows that One) as God, is liberated from the fetters of joy and sorrow" (Katha Upanishad, part II, XII).

On August 5, 2020, it was barely past midnight when I awakened. Spirit was downloading sentences into my mind, synthesizing my discoveries, helping me write my book. I took dictation as the words flowed out.

> *What I found through all my research was that Spirit was infused in everything I touched or examined. It mattered not if it was ancient, historical, or new. There is no barrier except in the minds of men. We are all One, and science now confirms that reality. Look to the stars, the numbers, the crystals, the elements of nature, the sciences, the sages, and you will find the thread of connection. Search the sand of the sea, read the face of the sky, or hear the breath of the air; it is all One.*
>
> *Portions of the One are in the fragments of truth that evolved into separate religions. The One displays itself in unbridled truth throughout the galaxies; there is no limit, no barrier, no separation, no difference. Science confirms we are made of the same stuff stars are made of.*
>
> *I laugh at myself, remembering how I searched through countless books, thinking that there must be one book that would answer all my questions. Humans have found it impossible to know everything about the One. What a miracle we are, for within us is the gateway that allows us to be aware of the One. We have access to what we need to know when we need to know it. This higher consciousness is above anything found in manuscripts ancient or new.*

※

My dear world family,

May you be blessed and strong in your journey. May you find and trust the light within to guide you. May your light shine and bring joy to others. Remember you are loved, and you are not alone. I will see you all on the other side.

Love and hugs, your sister,
Diana

Acknowledgments

I am very grateful to my editor, Lorraine Anderson, for helping me sculpt a lifetime of experiences into book form. I could not have asked for a better editor. From beginning to end, your exceptional skills, patience, and intuition helped me craft my story. You were always in sync with me as you polished, organized, and lifted the script to its best level.

I am indebted to Debra Stangl, founder of Sedona Soul Adventures, and to staff member Veronika Grace, who coordinated the soul adventure that transformed my life for the better. Debra, thank you for following your guidance and providing this service to souls in need. Veronika, you chose the perfect healing practitioners to meet my needs. Their combined gifts opened new portals to the spirit realm for me, and they planted the seeds of encouragement to write this book. I am eternally grateful.

Special thanks to Christina Pratt, founder of Last Mask Center for Shamanic Healing. Your ability as a shaman provided me with one of the most precious experiences of my life. The reuniting and integration that followed my soul retrieval session was profound and had lasting effects. Thank you for dedicating yourself to this work. It is a great service.

To my steadfast friends Deby and Tracy Beaty, I thank you for being with me through my traumas and my victories. I am so grateful for all your help and encouragement, as well as the ongoing meal exchanges at your home and mine. Without you, the darkest hours would have been nearly intolerable. You gave me something to look forward to and supported me without judgment during my evolution.

My darling child, Britney, you gave me reason to keep going and graciously cheered me on as well. You are a gift. I thank you and love you so much.

References and Recommended Reading

Borg, Marcus. *Meeting Jesus Again for the First Time*. New York: HarperCollins, 1994.

Dispenza, Joe. *Breaking the Habit of Being Yourself*. Carlsbad, CA: Hay House, 2012.

———. *Becoming Supernatural*. Carlsbad, CA: Hay House, 2017.

Dowling, Levi H. *The Aquarian Gospel of Jesus the Christ*. New York: Tarcher/Penguin, 2009. Originally published in 1908.

Fox, Matthew. *Original Blessing*. New York: Tarcher/Putnam, 2000. Originally published in 1983 by Bear & Company.

Giles, Keith. *Jesus Undefeated: Condemning the False Doctrine of Eternal Torment*. Orange, CA: Quoir, 2019.

Hay, Louise L. *You Can Heal Your Life*. Carlsbad, CA: Hay House, 1987.

Hicks, Esther and Jerry. *Ask and It Is Given*. Carlsbad, CA: Hay House, 2005.

Morter, Dr. Sue. *The Energy Codes*. New York: Simon and Schuster, 2019.

Moss, Robert. *Conscious Dreaming*. New York: Three Rivers Press, 1996.

———. *The Three "Only" Things*. Novato, CA: New World Library, 2007.

———. *Dreaming the Soul Back Home*. Novato, CA: New World Library, 2012.

Nelte, Frank W. "80 Mistranslations in the Bible and Their Significance." franknelte.net, April 2009.

Newton, Michael. *Journey of Souls*. Woodbury, MN: Llewellyn Publications, 1994.

———. *Destiny of Souls*. Woodbury, MN: Llewellyn Publications, 2007.

Pagels, Elaine. *The Gnostic Gospels*. New York: Random House, 1979.

Peirce, Penney. *The Intuitive Way*. Hillsboro, OR: Beyond Words, 1997.

Peng, Robert, *The Master Key*. Boulder, CO: Sounds True, 2014.

Shroyer, Danielle. *Original Blessing*. Minneapolis, MN: 2016.

Stangl, Debra. *The Journey to Happy*. Irvine, CA: Abundant Press, 2016.

Stevenson, Ian, MD. *Twenty Cases Suggestive of Reincarnation*, second edition. Charlottesville, VA: University Press of Virginia, 1974.

Sunfellow, David. *Love the Person You're With*. Sedona, AZ: David Sunfellow, 2016.

U.S. Catholic interview with Elizabeth Johnson. "No One Had to Die for Our Sins." *U.S. Catholic*, 27 November 2018.

Villoldo, Alberto. *The Four Insights*. Carlsbad, CA: Hay House, 2007.

Vitale, Joe. *Zero Limits*. Hoboken, NJ: Wiley, 2007.

Walsch, Neale D. *The Complete Conversations with God*. New York: Hampton Roads and G. P. Putnam's Sons, 2005.

Weir, Bill. "'Nobody Goes to Hell': Minister Labeled a Heretic." ABC News, 13 July 2007.

Yogananda, Paramahansa. *Autobiography of a Yogi*. Nevada City, CA: Crystal Clarity Publishers, 1990. Originally published in 1946.

Yukteswar, Swami Sri. *The Holy Science*, eighth edition. Los Angeles: Self-Realization Fellowship, 1990. Originally published in 1894.

Weiss, Brian L., MD. *Many Lives, Many Masters*. New York: Simon & Schuster, 1988.

Wendt, Sharon J. *The Radiant Heart.* Munster, IN: Radiant Heart Press, 1995.

The lyrics "How could anyone ever tell you you were anything less than beautiful? How could anyone ever tell you you were less than whole?" are from "How Could Anyone" by Libby Roderick, © 1988. The lyrics "It's a joy to get to know you" are from the song of the same name by Nicole Milner, © 1972. Both can be found on the CD by Shaina Noll titled *Songs for the Inner Child* (1994).

The Lost Years of Jesus is a 1977 film directed by Richard Bock.

Diana's Videos

Mark & Diana Wedding Highlights
www.youtube.com/watch?v=-WkEC32PWlo

Mark Schmidt Memorial
www.youtube.com/watch?v=uLAbKy06dEM

Crystal's Routine
www.youtube.com/watch?v=Q84moVv4cPA

About the Author

Diana Brown Schmidt was born and raised on a farm outside the small town of Sandy, Oregon. She played in the forest and developed a deep love for the beauty of nature, a love she has expressed in her artwork (which can be viewed at fineartamerica.com/profiles/3-diana-schmidt). She became an evangelical Christian at age sixteen and made a deep commitment to follow Jesus. Traumatic life events prompted Diana to recognize that she had unwittingly given away her power while deferring to religious doctrines and the opinions of others. Through the guidance of Spirit, she overcame her fears and found herself again. In *Jump Without Fear*, her voice calls to all, Don't silence your uniqueness. You, too, have a gift that our world needs. Her story is a call to unity, to love yourself and all others.

Made in United States
North Haven, CT
11 August 2022